Keeping Your Child Safe on Social Media

Anne McCormack

ABOUT THE AUTHOR

Anne McCormack is a psychotherapist based in Dublin. With over fifteen years' experience working with families and young people, she is an expert on how social media has changed the landscape when it comes to parenting young people and supporting them to stay mentally well. Anne is passionate about adolescent mental health and is keenly aware of both the positive and negative influence of social media in the lives of young people. Anne spoke at the inaugural Zeminar event in Dublin's RDS in 2016 on the issue of young people, consent and our need to speak more openly about pornography. She writes for the *Irish Times* and *A Lust for Life* and her work has featured in the *Irish Independent* and *HerFamily.ie* as well as in academic publications.

To link with Anne on social media:

Facebook: /anne.mccormack.71
Twitter: @MentalFitnessXX
Website: www.annemccormack.ie

KEEPING YOUR CHILD SAFE ON SOCIAL MEDIA

Five Easy Steps

Anne McCormack

ORPEN PRESS

Published by
Orpen Press
Upper Floor, Unit K9
Greenogue Business Park
Rathcoole
Co. Dublin
Ireland
email: info@orpenpress.com
www.orpenpress.com

Paperback ISBN 978-1-78605-018-2
ePub ISBN 978-1-78605-019-9
Kindle ISBN 978-1-78605-020-5
PDF ISBN 978-1-78605-021-2

Printed in Dublin by SPRINTprint Ltd

For Roisín, Malachy and Bronagh. Enjoy social media. x

To young people who have told me
you feel worthless …
Even if you only felt it for a moment, know that it's not true.

Feeling worthless is a feeling.

It is not a fact.

Acknowledgements

To my family for their endless support, patience and love. To Orpen Press for giving a life to my book. To the people who choose to share their journey of therapy with me and, in so doing, make me realise over and again how lucky I am to get to do the work I do. I am extremely grateful and indebted to you all.

TABLE OF CONTENTS

Table of Contents

Table of Contents

INTRODUCTION

'The choices we make are ultimately our own responsibility.'

Eleanor Roosevelt

PARENTING AND SOCIAL MEDIA

Social media, the collection of websites and applications that allows for online communication and content sharing, is an integral part of young people's lives. When it comes to parenting around technology use many parents can feel a bit lost about what the best course of action is. This is understandable because the parents of today did not grow up having access to modern technology or social media. So choices around the best way to parent can feel limited, because a whole new type of parenting is required. We all know how great social media can be, but we also are well aware of the potential danger. As a parent, you can tend to feel a bit at sea when it comes to questions such as:

- The best age to allow your child start using social media
- The best way to supervise or monitor your child's use of social media
- Whether you need to prepare your child for what they may have to face online and how to do this
- How to ensure your child does not feel the need to be online all the time

Young people join social media sites at a totally different stage of development to us adults. That is stating the obvious but it is a vitally important fact to bear in mind when you start thinking about your child and social media. Young people are not equipped with an adult mind and so they absolutely need to do preparatory work before going online in order to protect themselves and stay emotionally healthy.

For parents, not having experienced social media growing up means it can be hard to recognise what it is that young people face when social media becomes a big part of their life. As a psychotherapist I meet caring, diligent parents who cannot understand how their child has had to face such trouble and anguish because of their online activities and interactions. Some parents are shocked by how little they know about what their child was doing online. For young people, it is not safe for their parents to be so out of the loop.

We need to start early when it comes to preparing young people for social media and we need to see the social media part of our children's life as an aspect that we as parents remain involved in. In the same way that you get involved in your child's formal education by staying linked in with schoolwork, homework and how your child is getting on socially with friends, you can guide and support your child on their journey with social media too. You can be a mentor to your child on social media, supporting them to make good choices and manage difficulties right up until they reach adulthood or even a bit beyond. The conversations with our young people about social media need to begin before ever they are handed a mobile device. This is what is optimal for them.

Strict versus Lenient Parenting: Which Is Best?

Social media is just one more way in which people interact these days and it has become, for many, an essential part of everyday life. Social media has become as much a part of people's routine as eating or drinking but because young people are starting out on social media at a very different stage of development from those of us who started using social media as adults, there is a really urgent need for parents to be tuned in to how ready and able their child is for that complex social environment. Many of us wonder whether it is best to let our children go it alone on social media or try to monitor them closely. While some parents don't supervise or monitor their child's online use enough, this can sometimes simply be because parents feel unsure about the technology, what the apps are and how to use them. Monitoring and supervision is an essential part of parenting around social media, especially when young people are starting out on the social media journey. You need to be familiar and informed about social media sites before letting your child use them, but you also need to help your children develop the skills and resources to stay mentally well online.

Why is monitoring not enough? Young people can find ways to get around strict rules and there are some apps that allow users to hide their content as soon as it is uploaded. Even if supervision is tight to start with, as your child grows older they will begin to make online decisions by themselves. This is appropriate; it is how 'growing up' works. As young people grow, they want more independence and it is important for them to get that. But this wish and inevitable need for increasing independence points to the necessity of young people needing to be prepared from the inside out if they are to manage well on social media.

Being extremely strict when parenting around social media could lead to a point where your child starts to keep secrets from you and does things behind your back. And yet lenient parenting and lack of supervision and monitoring poses risks too as young people may feel free to explore whatever arouses their interest and curiosity, even if it poses obvious dangers. The key is to find a middle path, ensuring you have sensible limits on your children's social media use and having awareness of their online activity, while still respecting their privacy, fostering their independence and acknowledging that social media is an important part of a young person's world today.

Preparing your child for managing their online presence is about more than teaching them how to protect their physical safety. Telling them not to post their address is essential but it is not the kind of lesson that teaches them how to manage their emotional well-being. Emotional well-being needs to be protected too and there are simple steps you can take as part of a preparation plan to build your child's resilience. Once you know how to prepare your child for social media and support them to mind themselves while on it, the risk to their physical and mental well-being is reduced. I have met many young people who have ended up cutting themselves because of something that happened online. I know young people who feel worthless when comparing themselves to the social media influencers they adore and follow online. And these are young people who have caring and considerate parents. They are often young people too who have felt they could not burden their parents with their emotional pain, perhaps believing that their parents wouldn't 'get it'.

By reading this book, my hope is that you will become aware of how much power you have in protecting your children as they grow up in an online environment. These five easy steps will support young people to develop a high level of mental fitness which will help them stay emotionally strong online.

CONSEQUENCES OF TOO MUCH ONLINE USE

Many young people, once they start using social media, can end up spending a lot of time on it. One of the consequences of this can be that they spend less time on schoolwork and interacting with family, and they can prefer to be online than out playing sport or engaging in activities. Apart from this change of routine, there is another layer of change that may be going on – the change that can be happening inside the young person's mind.

Often, it is only when mental health problems become serious that symptoms really begin to be seen. So it is important to tune into how frequent social media use can impact on mental health. Mental health is closely linked to self-esteem and self-worth. As social media can sometimes create a risk to self-esteem, young people need to shore up their sense of self-worth so they have it as a resource if times get tough. They need to have information about how being online for hours on end can create a dependence on it and it can influence how they start to think about themselves. How this happens is discussed in detail in the following chapters. There are risks and by talking about them awareness is increased. My experience as a family psychotherapist has taught me that communicating early about any issues that may pose a risk is the best way to help young people learn how to mind themselves online.

THE TEENAGE YEARS AND SOCIAL MEDIA

It is important to realise that young people using social media sites are at a very different stage of development in their minds to adults.

Therefore, their experience of social media is going to be massively different and they will have unique challenges to face. Social media serves a different function for young people than it does for adults. Parents need to understand why this is.

Young people of eight, nine, ten years of age, or even pre-teens and teenagers, are not mature enough to be sure of who they are or what values they hold dear. Part of growing up means working this stuff out and so the question needs to be asked about how this 'working it out' publicly online may impact on them. This question about the level of maturity of the child is more relevant the younger the child. Many pre-teens are on social media sites. They haven't had the chance at that stage to really work out what matters to them and where they fit into the world around them. They are at the stage of development where they are still considered to be in need of supervision in the school yard as they interact socially with peers. They are malleable and open to manipulation because of their age and can often try to do and say what they think others may like much more than they would at an older age.

To a much greater extent than adults, children and young teens can tend to believe what they hear. This gullibility makes them more vulnerable than adults when it comes to what they view online and so they need to be supported to manage this. Some young people develop mental health difficulties while spending large amounts of time online and this can go largely unnoticed as mental health is not clearly visible when you just look at someone. Someone can become obsessive about their weight or appearance and the selfie culture can serve to exacerbate this issue for some. Low self-esteem or a constant need to get 'likes' can become debilitating for some young people if they are not prepared to handle well the social media environment. But negative outcomes such as these can largely be avoided if the child's mind is prepared and then supported along the way.

Social Media and Young Minds

Social media has become a massive part of teenage culture, and a major part of how young people connect with each other and the wider world. Because this is the case, young people who are not allowed any access to social media can feel as if their experience of the world is compromised. The social media world, because it can be fun and interesting, can become a place where young people wish to spend a lot of their time. This brings them out of the real world and into the cyber world with a vast amount of content. As their minds are at such a delicate stage of development, the young person needs support and preparation in order to build up resilience and strength to manage this content that they are being bombarded with. Children's minds are not yet strong in the way an adult mind can be. A child's identity has not yet had a chance to develop the way an adult's identity has and this is true even for children who seem full of confidence and strength.

MENTAL FITNESS AND MIND STRENGTH

Mental fitness is about keeping your emotional health in tip-top shape and the more a young person knows how their mind is working, how they can hold onto their confidence and how they can manage how they feel, the more they will be in charge of their own mental well-being. With an internal source of strength in the mind, your child will be much better able to cope with any challenges they face, such as dealing with exclusion, being ridiculed or peer pressure to portray themselves in a certain way. Mind strength makes young people mentally fit and mental fitness leads to resilience. This strength that develops inside the young person's mind becomes part of them. Therefore it is a real resource they can use when times get tough. This mind strength puts your child more in charge of how they see things and how they interpret things. It puts them in a better position to mind their mental health. Having strength in their mind gives your child better options about how to think. They are less vulnerable then during times when they may be about to jump to a bad conclusion about something. For example, if they read online about the latest craze in terms of what is deemed to be an attractive body shape, they will have the power to pause and not get so sucked into thinking this is gospel truth (which could make them feel bad), and they will be more likely to be able to monitor how they feel and why, and then change this feeling to something more healthy.

Digital Natives

Young people can easily navigate social media sites. Being a digital native means that they use computers and technology in the way that we all speak our mother tongue. We know the language we speak without question, without thought. Many young people today know technology that well too. They are growing up with it. They learn quickly at a young age about touchscreen technology and can easily navigate and access sites and apps they are curious to see. Children, before ever they go near social media, have often had experience of technology in the form of games and entertainment. And despite the fact that they may have information on cyber-bullying and what to do if a stranger tries to contact them, they also often have an expectation that social media is mostly a place to have fun and so they are not generally wary of it. While young people may be tech-savvy, it is a different set of skills that they need to cope with issues such as exclusion online, being harassed or not 'liked', or the experience of comparing themselves unfavourably over and over again to others. Sometimes the greatest threat to a person's mental health can be inside their own mind. Therefore, it is crucial to have good self-esteem and know specifically how to hold onto it while online.

An old African proverb states 'If there is no enemy within, the enemy outside can do no harm.' So if a young person has a strong mind before ever they go near social media, if they understand the benefit of mental fitness and if they are supported as they begin to use social media to hold onto that strength, they are in a much better position to cope with any adversity or threat that comes their way. Hence you need to tune into the notion of 'mind strength' and mental fitness and teach this to your children. Mental fitness is about good mental health going forward.

Young people do not automatically have the tools to maintain their mental resilience and strength online and they may not even see the need for these tools as they can be very focused on the positives aspects of social media use. Children are generally excited by the prospect of social media apps and parents can feel ill-equipped to even have a conversation with them about the need to know how to manage it all. Because children are not coming asking for support, parents can find it hard to offer it, even if they have a hunch that it's the right thing to do. It is not like the kind of situation where a child falls and hurt their knee and comes running for support. In that scenario, a plaster and a hug will do the trick. For social media issues, it can feel for parents as if the territory and their options are less clear.

Impulsivity

Difficulties can occur online not just because children are impressionable and gullible but because children, especially as the teenage years approach and continue, can be impulsive too. This combination can lead young people to behave online in ways that they think might make them look cool or popular, but may also be risky or offensive. Sometimes young people feel anxious or worried as they engage with others online. These feelings can come out of the blue for some and it can be difficult to work out how to deal with the feelings. This can at times lead some young people towards alcohol, drug use or self-harming behaviours as these harmful activities are sometimes used as a way to escape the difficult feelings. This is the reality when it comes to the environment our young people are growing up in. They need to be prepared to manage in this environment.

THE IMPORTANCE OF AGE RESTRICTIONS

As children grow towards the teenage years, they become more aware of the social media world. At an increasingly young age, children become familiar with the names of different popular social media sites such as Facebook or Snapchat. They may know that their image is online for many to see (on their parents' profiles) and they can't wait to take part in the social media 'action'. Children hear about social media sites from their friends or other children in school. Or they may be aware of the sites' existence because of a parent or sibling's frequent use of social media.

As social media is an integral part of life for most adults these days children have an expectation that they too will be socially active online as they grow older. However, parents differ in terms of the age at which they deem their child 'ready' for social media. It is almost always the child who comes looking for a device to allow them access to social media, rather than the parent encouraging them to get online. This is a point that parents can tune in to.

It is not for anyone to tell anyone else how to manage their child's online presence. Some might feel that to post images of their child online is ok, others feel it's not. As parents we all get to make choices for ourselves but, knowing that for many parents the decision regarding a child's social media access is simply about not wanting their child to feel left out if their friends are online prompts the following question for me: what would happen if all ten-year-olds started driving cars; would I feel pressure to let my ten-year-old drive a car just so they fit in and didn't feel that I was keeping them from being like everyone else? It may seem ludicrous to even contemplate such a far-fetched notion, and it is of course against the law for ten-year-olds to drive. But the point is about peer pressure that parents can feel. The dangers of allowing ten-year-olds to drive are apparent. But when it comes to ten-year-olds using social media, the water is a bit muddier for some parents. Personally, I would not let my ten-year-old on social media at all; I believe that twelve is young enough for children to start an online presence, but if parents feel peer pressure to do what other parents do (i.e. allow a child onto social media at a young age), then what sort of role modelling is going on when it comes to teaching young people about managing peer pressure? An alternative is to say to your child that they will be allowed on social media when you, as the parent, deem them to be ready and prepared. That approach can motivate young people then to begin to work on some of the ideas and exercises outlined in this book, as they will believe, if you do, that it is not safe for them to begin social media until they know their own mind better.

Adult-Only Sites

For some parents, it can be difficult to see any dangers at all with social media, particularly if you know your child's friends and it is those friends they will be interacting with online. It can seem harmless to let children interact online but that's an assumption that should not be made. Even if harm is not visible to the eye, harm can be lurking around. It is good to have knowledge of and pay attention to age restrictions for popular sites such as Facebook, Snapchat and Instagram. The age restrictions are there for good reason. These three sites require users to be thirteen years or over, and while there are many other social media sites particularly geared towards children, children often want to be on the sites that everyone else they know are on. Parents can feel that the age restrictions are too restrictive and so let their children on these sites with their consent. It can seem like an easy decision to just let a child use a social media site that is not specifically for their age, but this indirectly is giving the child the message that it is ok to lie about their age. At a later stage, for example, when the child is sixteen and wanting to access an adult social media site for eighteen-year-olds, the dangers posed can seem suddenly so much more real for parents if the site is one that contains porn. And yet if the young person has been allowed to lie about their age previously, they may feel justified to lie about their age once again. What position do parents then find themselves in if they are trying to explain to their sixteen-year-old how dangerous and inappropriate an adult site such as Fuckbook or Pornostagram is? Young people hear about adult sites from peers, often in early adolescence. Even if these sites are not being talked about at home, young people know they exist. And these sites are dangerous places for young people to be hanging about.

Young people start hearing about social media porn sites at an age where they are becoming increasingly interested in sex. If you don't know how to handle this issue of the accessibility of pornography on mobile devices, it can trigger a perfect storm. When making a decision about allowing your children to start using social media sites, you need to be linking these decisions to ones you will need to face in the future.

SOCIAL MEDIA SITES AND PROTECTION: GETTING YOUR CHILD STARTED

There are different things you can do if you wish to slowly begin to allow your child onto social media sites in a supported way. You could start by allowing your child access the chosen social media site on a shared home computer situated in a shared space, such as a kitchen or living room (not their bedroom). You can then be in the room while your child is online and you can chat to them about how they are interacting with their friends, who they are in touch with and how they are getting on. This is a different type of parenting approach to simply monitoring from afar. It involves a supportive 'I've got your back if it gets difficult' layer and you want your child to be aware of this layer from the start. You want your child to know that you don't want to spy on their activities but you are there to guide and support them. Once you feel your child is ready they may start using a smartphone, tablet or other handheld device. Although this enables them to go online without direct supervision, you can still monitor and support them. You can request that your child shares all passwords with you so that you can check their online activity. If your child is not willing to share the passwords, you can absolutely take steps to curtail their access to the internet or social media. You can also introduce a rule that all mobile devices are to be turned off at night and kept out of bedrooms. Whatever approach is used, it is important that you remain aware of how the approach you are taking is impacting on your relationship with your child. One way to do this is to simply ask them. And even if you monitor your child's activity, they could still be at risk because of what they face online. Filtering devices alone are not enough. Preparation of the child's mind is essential.

WHY DOES MENTAL FITNESS MATTER SO MUCH?

Often young people are at crisis point by the time they tell anyone how difficult things are for them online. I know from my clinical experience that increasing a young person's level of mental fitness, increasing secure attachment and preparing them to deal with difficult emotions will protect them well online. If the preparatory work is done, young people are much less likely to ever reach crisis point in the first place.

No one style of parenting fits for everyone and this is true when it comes to parenting around social media also. The important thing is to ensure that your children get the following message loud and clear about social media: it is something they need to be prepared for if they are to manage it well. If they don't prepare, they can encounter difficult situations that can cause them harm or it can become a place where they cause harm to someone else. When it comes to young people and social media, mental fitness matters.

WHO IS THIS BOOK FOR?

This book is for parents of children and teens who are already using social media or who will be using social media sometime in the future. It is also for teachers and others who interact with young people around social media use. It can be used to help you work out how to support the child or teenager to gain mental fitness so that they are emotionally and psychologically prepared to deal with social media and the potential dangers it poses. It is a guide to preparing young people for social media by focusing on five easy steps. And it gives clear insight into why preparing young people's minds is a necessary endeavour.

WHY READ IT?

By reading this book, parents and teachers will know how to prepare young minds for social media and also why this absolutely needs to happen. By following the five steps outlined in this book, you can support young people to build resilience to cope well within the social media world. Any difficult experiences they may encounter online will have much less negative impact if the young person is mentally fit. And while social media can be really positive and a lot of fun, and while it has wonderful resources that young people can access, bad things can happen to anyone. As a parent you cannot be in control of how others may treat your child online but following these five steps will help to protect their happiness and confidence online.

WHAT DOES THIS BOOK CONTAIN?

This book contains five easy steps to take to prepare your child's mind for social media, broken into two sections. Section I (Gaining Mental Fitness), covering Steps One to Three deals with work that can be done with your child before they go online or once they are active online. Section II (Managing When Times Get Tough), covering Steps Four and Five, focuses on what to do if times get tough, but it is best to cover this before that happens so that if your child does face problems they will know what to do. Section II contains (fictional) case studies which can be used at your own discretion. If your child has been on social media for a while and they are old enough to work through the specific examples outlined then you can work through this second section of the book with them. Some of the examples are not suitable for young children to work through and so parental discretion is advised.

Step One: Understanding Mind Development

This chapter looks at how an understanding of the stage of development the young person is at directly relates to their desire to be on social media. It also explains some young people's seeming need to feel 'liked' and admired by peers. When parents understand mind development, they are in a much better position to appropriately support their growing adolescent on social media.

Think of parents of toddlers who understand the toddler's physical developmental stage. For toddlers, this physical developmental stage involves the task of learning to walk and talk. Once parents know this is the stage of their (physical) development, they can provide useful and appropriate support. Perhaps holding their hand as they try to stand up or repeating back the proper pronunciation of a word they are attempting to say would come naturally to a parent who knows what physical 'task' the child is dealing with. And that is how it is for teenage mind development too. Understanding mind development matters so much for parents of young people. It is key for parents who wish to understand and appropriately support their growing child. Understanding mind development and the 'task' the young person is facing in their mind and then sharing some of this knowledge with the young person themselves is one of the foundations for supporting young people to understand themselves and hence stay happy and confident on social media.

Step Two: Understanding Confidence and Its Sources

Social media is a very public space to be and while this public aspect of the social media world may be an attractive idea to many young people, confidence is a critical part of what they need to manage well there. Confidence can be knocked quite quickly online and young people need to learn how to manage this. If young people lack confidence in the first place, or if their confidence is quite good but is reliant to a large extent on feedback from others, they can be vulnerable online. This section explains how parents can support children to develop healthy and sustainable confidence.

Step Three: Making Attachment Secure

In Step Three, the focus is on attachment and how to ensure this attachment is secure. Secure attachment has been shown to help reduce the level of depression, anxiety and self-harm among young people. It is linked to the well-being of any young person online and it has a bearing on all aspects of their behaviour, including sexual behaviour.

Step Four: Knowing How to Manage Difficult Emotions

Impulsivity is a normal part of adolescence but impulsivity can create difficulties for some on social media. This is particularly true if the young person has heightened emotions such as sexual arousal or a high level of anger or hurt. Other difficult feelings arise in situations where young people are excluded, ridiculed, let down or humiliated. It can be difficult to deal with the intensity of feeling that comes and because young people are often on social media sites when they are alone, they need to learn how to look after themselves if they get over-whelmed. Some young people turn to alcohol, drugs or self-harming as a way to escape the pain of difficult emotion. They need to know how to keep safe. In this chapter, the focus is on teaching young people to pause and identify their feelings and thoughts and to consider their beliefs before taking action.

Case studies are used in this chapter to facilitate discussion about things that can go wrong. While social media can be a very positive aspect of a young person's life, and encountering difficulties is not inevitable, it's good to be prepared. Working through these case studies with your teenager can alert them to ways in which things can go wrong. It also provides the opportunity to explore positive ways of coping.

Step Five: How to Recover if Things Go Wrong

It can be hard to work out what to do to best support young people when tough times come their way. In Step Five, case studies are again used to outline how young people can be supported to recover from difficult times. These serve to:

- Outline for parents some of the things that can end up happening to young people on social media sites
- Offer insight into how to avoid these situations occurring
- Point to ways to help a young person recover if the difficulty does arise

It can be hard for parents to imagine what can go wrong online, unless they find themselves in the unfortunate position of having to pick up the pieces after something goes wrong. And things can go wrong for any young person, even if their parents are exceptionally hard-working when it comes to parenting. Some parents like to think that nothing bad will happen to their child on social media but things happen sometimes to those who least expect it. It is best not to take any chances. It is best to be prepared.

Note: Some of the content in the case studies would not be suitable to share with young teens. Use your own discretion.

SECTION I

GAINING MENTAL FITNESS

1

Step One: Understanding Mind Development

'Until you make the unconscious conscious, it will direct your life and you will call it fate.'

C.G. Jung

Understanding Mind Development: Understanding the Unconscious

With some aspects of development, it is clear that it is happening. Take physical development. The body of a baby clearly differs from that of a teenager and therefore the change that happens is obvious. Mental development is different in that we can't see into another person's mind. It is hard to see how someone is developing inside their mind and even for the person themselves it can be difficult to understand because their own mind is largely invisible to them, unless they have studied psychology. Within the mind, a lot happens under the surface: in the subconscious, or at a deeper level again, at an unconscious level. This means that the person themselves, unless they are digging down under the surface of their mind, will not be aware of what is going on there. And yet it is the deepest level, the unconscious part of the mind, which, to a large extent, directs a person's motives, moods and behaviours. This is what Carl Jung meant when he said that the unconscious, if left unexplored, will direct your life. It is as true for any of us as it is for teenagers. In this first step, the aim is to shed light on what is happening in a young person's unconscious mind. That way, you are more aware of and can better understand your child's motives, feelings and behaviours. You are also then equipped with knowledge you can give your child in order to enable them to be more aware of how their mind is impacting on how they feel online. This then will help them cope better with their own experiences online. For example, if a young person is determined to get a certain amount of 'likes' for their selfie and they have information about the task they are facing deep down in their mind, it really helps. This is because the mental task the young person is facing is that of working out their identity. Because this task is in their unconscious mind, they are only aware of it if they are told about it. This task can make them highly sensitive to feedback from others, which can be a major part of why getting so many 'likes' matter. If a young person is told, 'You are working out your identity deep down in your mind and that can make you really interested in, and sensitive to, feedback from others, so mind yourself and pay attention to how you are interpreting the feedback', it builds their resilience for life online.

What Is Mind Development?

It is important to remember that as we grow, the mind develops and matures, just as our bodies do. Think of all the physical changes that occur as a baby becomes a toddler, a child becomes an adolescent, and finally an adolescent becomes an adult. Because the body is something we can see, the changes that happen to it are more easily understood. Now switch your focus onto a person's mind. It cannot be readily seen and that makes it harder to know what changes are happening. It is not even always clear that change is happening when it cannot be observed. But change does happen in the mind. And just as we face physical challenges in order to grow and develop, we face psychological challenges too. For young people using social media, they may be tech-savvy in a way that makes parents stand back in awe. But this ability to use technology is not in any way a reflection of the young person's ability to think in complex ways about themselves or relationships, and it doesn't equip them to deal with complex social situations. Children and adolescents think differently to adults and that is because they are at a different stage of development. Their minds are very different. One example of this was confirmed by a research study published by Ofcom in November 2015. The study found that young teens were largely unaware that bloggers they follow on YouTube were being paid to advertise products. Young people were found to be totally trusting of everything they saw on the web, and not able to decipher between fiction and fact. Adults are, generally speaking, much less inclined to be that naive. Adults are generally more discerning when it comes to what they believe. This is an example of how children can be potentially put at risk, because of their less developed and more gullible minds.

While every person's body is unique and individual, there is a definite, observable pattern in terms of how it changes as they grow. Think of a toddler and their physical development. They each learn to walk and talk at a different rate while also following a certain norm or pattern. There is a normal range within which physical development happens; usually young babies and toddlers are checked by health professionals to ensure this development is happening within the 'normal' range. We change and grow in a standard pattern and the same is true of the mind. This is called psychological development.

For adolescents, physical development is still taking place. But the psychological development taking place is particularly relevant as they engage with social media. This development relates to what the young person's mind is grappling with, and it usually happens without them being aware of it. By understanding this development you, as parents, can become aware of how it can impact what happens when your child joins the social media world. You can then educate your child about how their mind is working. This is a vital step towards keeping them safe and building up their mental fitness.

There is a particular mind task facing young people as they go through the teenage years and that is the task of working out their identity, which is explored in more detail below. If you understand what this mind task is, you are able, to some extent at least, to see into your child's mind and, therefore, tailor your support to optimise the chances that they will stay happy and confident online. With a toddler, parents may provide a supportive hand and words of encouragement to help them learn to walk, because they know that this is what the toddler is trying to do; it is 'normal' development. With adolescence, knowing what is 'normal' mental development aids parents to better understand and help their children. Without appropriate support, it can become hard for adolescents to develop confidence and a sense of their own worth. They can fall into the trap of seeking 'likes' in order to feel validated and that is not good for their self-esteem as it hands power over to others. Parents can provide support that is useful in combating this risk of low self-worth. And it is worthwhile to do this as low self-worth is a potential risk to a child's mental health and can add to their vulnerability online. For example, if your child is following celebrities on social media, it is worth checking with them whether they ever compare themselves to that celebrity and how that impacts on their self-esteem. This brings the issue up into the conscious part of their mind, the part that they can know and have control over. It is important to say to your child that comparing themselves to others can be a normal part of working out their identity. But it is also important to say that comparing themselves to others who post images online that are extremely glamourous and polished can leave them either feeling pressure to look similar or feeling a bit unhappy with themselves. It is important that young people don't fall into the trap of thinking that these images on social media are a reflection of real people. Real people are about more than a physical image and, a lot of the time, the image is digitally manipulated anyway.

At different ages we face different tasks in our minds, but most people are not aware of these tasks and so a lot of what happens in the unconscious mind is never fully understood. Erickson (1997) wrote extensively about the tasks we face in our unconscious mind. Our minds are like icebergs. With an iceberg, you only ever see the bit that is above water, which is a small amount of the total iceberg. The mind is similar to this, in that most people only ever know part of what is in their mind: the part that is accessible and known, which is referred to as the conscious mind. This conscious mind represents the part of the mind that you have awareness of. An example of this awareness is knowing that you are thinking about what you have planned for later today, or thinking about something that has just been said to you. It includes thoughts such as 'I'm so hungry, I'm really looking forward to having breakfast' or 'I cannot believe she just said that; I would not speak to anyone that way.' Such conscious thoughts are easily known to the person thinking them. But all sorts of things happen much deeper down in our minds; this is also the place where core beliefs are stored. The part of the iceberg that is under water and cannot be seen makes up the bulk of the iceberg. This unconscious mind strongly influences how a person feels and how they may behave. When you do not know what is going on in that part of your mind however, you are not aware of how much it is influencing you. So to have more control over how you feel or act, it is vital to know what is going on in the unconscious part of your mind. Knowing yourself well brings the unconscious up into the conscious mind and knowing the mind task you face at any given time is a way to bring something from the unconscious mind up into the conscious part where you are then more in charge of it, simply because you know about it. Once the mind task of identity formation faced by your adolescent is known by you, the parents, you can explain it to your child. You can explain, for example, that feedback from others, especially peers or people they don't know yet and so haven't had feedback from before, really matters as this feedback can translate into new information about themselves which in turn helps them work out their identity. For example, a Facebook friend request from someone they don't know can tell them something about themselves. A friend request from a stranger might be interpreted as 'They like my profile picture so that tells me that I look well.' When young people know this task is being faced by them, they can understand better why they may feel interested in interacting with strangers online (in order to get feedback) and once this awareness about themselves is known, they will be in a better position to then have a conversation about the possible dangers of interacting with strangers online. When the mind task remains unknown to both parents and young people such conversations about interacting with strangers online can seem to fall on deaf ears as the young person can feel 'Mum/Dad doesn't get it'; this can be true but the young person also doesn't get why they are so interested in feedback from strangers. As more is brought up into the conscious part of the mind, more becomes visible and, therefore, influence over the mind is expanded. A person becomes mentally fitter and stronger when they have increased awareness of their own mind. The more young people know about this task of identity formation, the more they can be in charge of making their mind work for them, rather than against them.

What Are Mind Tasks?

As with physical development challenging us to learn to walk, talk, cycle, etc., we all face different mind tasks too, such as working out if we are capable of trusting others, or of loving others. These mental tasks happen at different stages of our life, depending on age. By becoming aware of what they are, a person then has a choice about how they wish to deal with each task. You cannot take your child's mind out of their head for them to see what is going on in there but you can give them information to understand their own mind better. When children are younger than ten, it is too complex an idea to try to teach them about mind tasks, but by the time adolescence is approaching young people would have the capacity to understand the idea of a mind task. Their mind can grasp the concept because it has developed enough to do this.

One theorist who has written extensively about the mind tasks facing people as they go through life is Erik Erikson. He describes eight different stages of psychological or mind development where we face eight challenges or questions in our (unconscious) mind. In the main, these are questions that remain in the unconscious mind for the vast majority of people. But by becoming conscious of them we can gain strength over our mind, i.e. mental fitness, and we gain more understanding of why we may feel certain things at various stages of life. Once you know the task you face, you can take charge to a greater extent.

The Sequence of Mind Tasks

Without learning to sit first, it would be difficult to manage standing. Without learning to walk, it would be really difficult to learn to run. So the learning happens in a sequence. The same is true for a person's mental development. For example, a child needs to work out how to operate within social rules and how to get along with others, which is why the school yard is so important. If this task is not completed successfully, that child, during adolescence, will find it harder to work out their identity because part of that task involves interacting with others in order to get feedback and using that feedback then to work out who you are in the world.

So if something difficult happens at a particular point in a person's life, this affects whether or not they complete the task they are facing successfully. If the task is not completed successfully, it can then impact on how they manage with the next task they have to face into. Imagine trying to run without having properly learned to walk. In order to help your child to be mentally fit and strong knowing the sequence can be very useful. Sometimes traumatic events impact on the unconscious mind. Sometimes though, even things that do not seem to be traumatic have a great influence on the mind, for example finding it hard to play with other children in the school yard. It may not seem traumatic but it can be damaging to the young child's successful completion of the mind task of working out how to get along with others. Experiences such as those can then impact on how a person's core beliefs about themselves and other people develop. Unless you pay attention to what a child's beliefs about themselves are, the beliefs can develop in a negative way and compromise mental fitness. For example, a person may develop a core belief that no one really likes them and they may not even be aware of this belief being there, deep down in their mind.

By successfully completing the mind tasks it is more likely that you will feel confident, content and mentally fit. It also makes it more likely that you will feel good in relationships, feel good on social media and feel good about your life in general. This is as true for parents as it is for young people.

However, successfully completing any one task does not mean you will automatically be successful in completing the others. At any point, a person can find a task difficult but what is most difficult for people is if they find a task hard to complete and then have to move onto the next one without knowing they have that struggle going on inside their mind. In this type of situation, difficulties can arise. For example, difficulties can impact negatively on a person's confidence and negative beliefs about themselves or the world can develop or become set. These beliefs then get brought into the next stage and can contribute to a person becoming anxious, depressed or ambivalent about their life. If a person is not aware of beliefs they hold about themselves, the beliefs can turn into facts in their mind. One result of this can be that a person loses hope about being in charge of their own destiny.

UNDERSTANDING THE STAGES OF PSYCHOLOGICAL DEVELOPMENT

What Are the 'Tasks' We Face in Our Mind?

We face mind tasks in a particular sequence, and Erik Erickson described these tasks as happening at eight different stages throughout our lives. These stages, according to Erickson's description, are:

- Stage 1: Trust versus mistrust
- Stage 2: Autonomy versus shame and doubt
- Stage 3: Initiative versus guilt
- Stage 4: Industry (competence) versus inferiority
- Stage 5: Identity versus role confusion (this is the key task addressed in this chapter)
- Stage 6: Intimacy versus isolation
- Stage 7: Generativity versus stagnation
- Stage 8: Ego integrity versus despair

Stage 1: Trust versus Mistrust

The first mind task is faced during infancy. Erikson called this the 'Trust versus Mistrust' stage and the main task of the infant child is to figure out the answer to the question 'Can I trust the world?' This is mainly solved (unconsciously) through the infant's interactions with their main carer from birth to about age two. Facial expressions from the main caregivers matter a great deal as they are one of the primary ways of communicating with an infant who is just beginning to learn language skills. For example, responding to a crying infant with warmth and love gives the infant the understanding that they are loved and therefore lovable. They will also begin to develop a sense that yes, they can trust this person to care for them and meet their needs. This belief then forms into a more general belief about being able to trust not just that one caregiver but the world in general. This mind task is obviously not known to the infant and, generally speaking, parents of infants don't know their babies are facing this task either. Despite this, the task is still being worked through by the infant's mind. If they come to the conclusion that yes, the world is 'safe', they have successfully completed the task. On the other hand, if an infant suffers high levels of neglect they will likely learn to face the world with mistrust.

Stage 2: Autonomy versus Shame and Doubt

The second stage occurs during the toddler years and is referred to as 'Autonomy versus Shame'. Children go through this stage from the age of approximately eighteen months to three years. Children of this age are trying to figure out the answer to the question 'Is it ok for me to do things, to act this way?' Children answer this (at an unconscious level) by beginning to move about and explore the world. The young child either concludes that yes, it is ok for them to explore, open doors, colour pictures, etc. because they are greeted with warmth and smiles as they do (in which case they feel autonomy) or it is not ok to move about and explore their physical environment as they are met with hostility and shouting, for example, every time they touch something or move around a room (in which case they can feel some shame). Parents are largely unaware of this task being faced by toddlers and yet they are often the people who help the child work through the task.

Stage 3: Initiative versus Guilt

From about three years of age until five years, children generally begin to take some initiative, perhaps asserting themselves more and making up games that they then suggest to other people. If a child at this stage receives a lot of criticism and is not supported in their initiatives in play and creativity they may feel guilt and be less inclined to take initiative. If they don't feel any guilt however and are allowed free reign to do exactly as they wish, this is also less than ideal as they will not learn about limits and self-control. It is important at this stage for children to experience a balance between feeling free to take initiative and feeling remorse or guilt if they take things too far. To be able to provide an environment for pre-schoolers where they begin to learn about boundaries while also taking initiative is optimal.

Stage 4: Industry (Competence) versus Inferiority

When children reach the age of about five years, they start the next stage of development and face the next mind task. This is the 'Industry v Inferiority' task. From five to about twelve years of age child are grappling with the question 'Can I make it in this world of people and things?' This is quite a broad question being worked out by a child of this age and the school environment and a child's experience of friendship are two of the things that help children work their answer out. Can they make it? I believe that introducing social media during this stage of development complicates the solving of the answer to this question and so feel that dealing with this task makes it difficult for children of this age to take on the complexities of social media relationships too. It is great if school life and the social life of children at this age are positive experiences for them as it gives them the opportunity to answer 'Yes, I can make it; I can work out how to get along with others in this world.' If the child develops confidence and has a sense of accomplishment, then the answer will be a resounding 'yes'. They will feel able to manage social situations and environments with rules and boundaries; they will feel industrious. This industrious feeling will most likely happen if the child manages to make friends in the yard, if they feel they can manage school work and games played with others. If, on the other hand, something happens to disrupt the development of this sense of accomplishment, this sense of 'I know how to do things and how to be around people', then it is very, very important to notice this and respond to it. Because children do not know they are facing this 'task' in their mind, they are not aware of how the outcome can impact on them. Parents need to be mindful of what beliefs children of this age are developing about themselves, the world and other people.

Incidences that can trigger problems on an unconscious level during this stage can include bullying, struggles with friends, feeling excluded or feeling like you don't know how to do things that you are expected to do. The child who goes through difficult times may be developing a sense of inferiority about themselves and will need support with this. They could be developing negative beliefs about themselves, such as 'I'm no good at this' or 'Nobody really likes me.' Because these beliefs are forming in the unconscious part of their mind the child may not be at all aware of them. Parents can intervene by checking with children about what they think (and believe) about themselves on a regular basis. A question such as 'What do you think makes you a good friend?' or 'Why do you think that you and Sarah get on well together?' can bring awareness to the child's successes in getting along with others. It is important that children are supported and encouraged so that they feel they are able to manage in their world (of school and friends mainly). If they do not believe they can do this, they may begin to feel inferior. This is something then that erodes confidence and so parents encouraging and praising their child minimises this risk. Because this task is complex for children, it is best that social media does not become part of their social environment until this psychological task is completed. Moving into the next stage of development is time enough for children to begin to use social media. And even if children are twelve or thirteen before they are engaging on social media, it is important for parents to be aware that this task of working out how to get along with others can be brought forward and faced still during adolescence if it has not been successfully resolved at an earlier age. Not only will the young person still be grappling with this task of 'Can I make it in this world of people, can I work out how to get along with others?', but they will also be beginning to face into the next task, with a lower than optimal level of confidence and self-worth.

Stage 5: Identity versus Role Confusion

According to Erikson, young people aged between twelve and eighteen years approximately are dealing with the task known as 'Identity versus Role Confusion'. The main question being grappled with at an unconscious level is 'Who am I and what am I like?' Part of working this out for many teenagers involves getting hooked on feedback from others. And aspects of this task can impact greatly on how they navigate the social media world. Being aware of and managing this clash between the task of identity formation faced during adolescence and the development of a teenager's social media experience is a central aspect of the first step in keeping your child safe on social media.

Stage 6: Intimacy versus Isolation

There is no absolute boundary between where adolescence ends and adulthood begins; some say adolescence in now stretching into the early twenties. Legally, once a person reaches the age of eighteen years they are considered to be an adult, but in terms of a person's mental development the task of identity formation can continue past the age of eighteen. Everyone is different and while there is a 'normal' range for mind development, there is no absolute time frame that determines where your child should be at. The stage of development after adolescence is known as the 'Intimacy versus Isolation' stage. This task, generally speaking, is dealt with in the period from 19 to 39 years of age. The main question being figured out on an unconscious level during these years is 'Am I capable of love/can I cope with intimacy?'

For many people it is during this period of time that they settle into longer-term couple relationships. In the process, they are answering 'yes' to their unconscious question: 'Yes, I am capable of love and intimacy.' During this time too, people often begin to think about and have children. Having children is a massively life-changing experience for many and this experience of having a child can cause people to answer, again, in their unconscious mind, 'Yes, I am capable of love.'

While committing to a long-term relationship and having children may be a common experience that causes a person of this age to reach the completion of the task in their mind, it is obviously not the only route to successful completion of this task. And even if the question is answered, it can resurface if you begin to question the relationship or the love or the experience of intimacy. This then can, for some, cause psychological distress.

Stage 7: Generativity versus Stagnation

The period of life from about 40 to 65 years of age is referred to by Erikson as the period when people deal with 'Generativity v Stagnation'. It is the period of time that many parents of teens start going through, and the unconscious question facing parents in this age bracket is 'Can I make my life count?' Because this question is being dealt with for many under the surface, unconsciously, people's awareness about the fact that their mind is dealing with this question can be extremely low. Therefore, parents can feel frustrated and sometimes stressed and low themselves, not knowing really the reasons why. It can be difficult to parent teens and life gets very busy. It can feel at times for parents that looking at the question of making their life count would be something that would take up too much time and would be a luxury, when so much busyness happens on a day-to-day basis. This task or question remains in the unconscious for parents until after their children become adults. Then, when there is perhaps more space in their minds for parents, this psychological question and its impact can surface more.

Stage 8: Ego Integrity versus Despair

The final stage of mind development is known as the period of 'Ego Integrity v Despair'. This stage starts to be faced by people when they reach the age of about 65 years. The main question faced at this stage is 'Is it ok to be me/to have been me?' With this question comes a sense of looking back and reflecting on how life has been so far. If a person feels their life has been generally ok, they will feel a sense of integrity and have more hope about how the future will be. If, on the other hand, a person feels regret and that their life hasn't been how they may now wish it to have been, they can feel despair. Despair is a difficult feeling to face but knowing about the task at least lets you know the context for understanding why this feeling may be present.

ADOLESCENCE AND IDENTITY FORMATION

What Does 'Identity Formation' Mean?

Stage 5, the task of identity formation, is the mind task being faced during adolescence. Identity formation means going through the process of working out who you are and what your identity is. A person's identity is made up of many aspects of who they are: the way they look, the way they interact with others, their personality, their abilities and talents, their values. Everyone works out their identity in a different way but for young people going through adolescence today there are many different messages in society influencing their ideas about what is deemed to be good and of value. Appearance is deemed to be of huge importance in Western culture today and this dominant idea about how much appearance matters is one that young people have to deal with constantly on social media.

Forming an identity happens mainly in the unconscious part of the mind, so young people are not consciously focused on thoughts such as, 'What do I think of myself today?' The clothes young people wear, the music they may listen to, the different peer groups they befriend, the amount of time they spend experimenting with their appearance/hair colour/make-up, etc. – these can all be seen as part of the process of working out their identity. However, if a young person finds it difficult to form an identity that works for them or that they feel good about they can experience an 'identity crisis'. Coined by Erikson, an identity crisis is defined as:

> A psychosocial state or condition of disorientation and role confusion occurring especially in adolescents as a result of conflicting internal and external experiences, pressures, and expectations and often producing acute anxiety.
>
> *The American Heritage Dictionary of the English Language,*
> fifth edition, 2016

So an identity crisis is largely an internal crisis, something which cannot be seen on the outside. An identity crisis can happen at any age but for adolescents the process of forming an identity is very central to their development.

'Who am I?' can be a hard question to work out the answer to. It can take time for a person to reach a conclusion about themselves and working it out can be complicated if the young person has not successfully completed the previous mind task (industry v inferiority). Young people can go onto social media sites holding a sense of inferiority about themselves. This can place them in a vulnerable position, for example wanting to please or seem cool to others in order to feel good about themselves. Making young people aware of the fact that they are facing this psychological task of identity formation on an unconscious level is part of what helps them stay strong. If an incident arises on social media, a young person who knows about the psychological task in their mind will be better able to say to themselves:

- How is this impacting on my sense of who I am?
- Does this make me question myself in any way?

And knowing what question is being grappled with during adolescence gives young people a better understanding of their own feelings and behaviours while online.

Why Is Social Media So Important to Adolescents?

Apart from the opportunity social media gives young people to connect with each other, it is important to acknowledge the fact that everyone wishes to feel of worth and of value. Everyone likes to be 'liked' and deemed of worth by others, but as you grow through adulthood it can matter less what others think of you once you have formed an identity and are secure in yourself.

During adolescence, when your unconscious mind is focused on trying to work out your identity (who am I?), it makes sense that it matters much more to know what others think of you. This is one of the reasons why social media seems to young people to offer them so much. Not only do they get to connect with others, they get to work out what others think of them and they also get to think about how they might be similar to or different from other people. They get to learn about the world but the world they learn about through social media can be extremely filtered and often shallow.

On social media young people can give feedback and therefore come to understand their own preferences and likes, which also helps identity formation. This feedback, giving it and receiving it, then presents young people with the opportunity to reflect on the question about what matters to them and what is important. This offers them insight only if they take time to reflect on it. Otherwise, they can become strongly influenced by messages they get online about what is important; their own values and individual attitudes to things can go largely undeveloped or ignored.

When young people know about this 'identity formation' task, they can actively think about what way their identity is forming and how they are interpreting feedback from others, and they can assess for themselves how much their thinking is being led by dominant ideas in society rather than their own minds.

An example may be a young person posting a selfie and then monitoring the amount of 'likes' it gets. By thinking about how the feeling they experience while waiting for likes (e.g. anxiety or excitement) is linked to the question 'Who am I?', they can monitor how much importance they are placing on the 'likes'. Thinking and reflecting about issues that exist in the unconscious mind leads to increased strength in the mind. Prompting them to think about how scenarios link to their identity formation will lead the young person to develop the habit of reflecting on their feelings, rather than being passive and just reacting to something that is unconscious. With awareness, they are in a better position to make a choice, and they can then choose not to care so much what others think, if they see that the way they are being 'evaluated' is not in line with their own values. For example, many young people who focus on being assessed by 'likes' given for their appearance may, if they reflect on it, seem shallow, and most young people would not wish to be shallow or choose to judge others in a shallow way. They may, upon reflection, see that they actually don't want to determine their worth by their physical image. By reflecting, they are at least giving themselves the choice not to focus so much on feedback on appearance, either their own or that of celebrities.

The Role of Parents in Helping Adolescents Work Out Their Identity

Parents have a vital role to play in educating, supporting, mentoring and role-modelling for their children as they go through adolescence. But adolescents, while working out their identity, can tend to create a distance between themselves and their parents. While this distance is understandable once you know that they are trying to work out their own identity, for parents it can feel like a rejection. It can also create tension as parents may feel the need to monitor and supervise more the more their child pushes them away.

If your children used to want to be close to you and share things with you it can feel as if they are becoming distant. But this is not about your child wanting to reject you; rather creating this distance is part of healthy 'identity forming' behaviour. Part of this process of identity formation may involve thinking thoughts such as 'Am I like my parents?', 'I am not like my parents' or 'Some aspects of me are different to how my parents are/think/behave or what my parents believe.'

Once you understand the process of identity formation your adolescent child is going through, the first step in keeping them safe on social media is to share this information with them so that they are aware of the struggle going on at an unconscious level. By doing this, you are acknowledging your child's wish to step away and create some space. You can acknowledge that this is healthy and normal while still staying connected in a supportive and mentoring way with what is going on in your child's life on social media. One way to do this explicitly is to acknowledge the distance and to normalise it by saying that you accept and understand it. Secure attachment is also of central importance here as it ensures the quality of the relationship between you and your child as they grow; the topic of secure attachment is the focus of Chapter 3. You can manage the space between you and your child while also keeping the relationship strong by:

- Reassuring your child that you understand what is happening in the relationship dynamic between you
- Reassuring them that any distance does not make you any less present in their life and that you are still there and available to them any time they need support
- Informing your child that the distance, while understandable and acceptable, needs to be managed and discussed from time to time, so that you still feel connected to each other and they still feel they can trust you
- Reassuring your child that the distance does not mean that you will love them or think about them any less and that you will still be there to listen without judgement to absolutely anything they wish to say

One obvious consequence of the psychological task of identity formation during adolescence is the young person's desire to be around and have contact with people of the same age. This is normal and it is appropriate as it is only by being around others and experiencing what it is like to experiment, express and converse that young people have the context to work out how they are different or similar to everyone else in their age bracket. One of the risks of social media for adolescents comes from the amount of time a young person spends comparing themselves favourably or unfavourably to others. Also, this need to be around people their own age can impact negatively on family relationships if young people want to be on social media all of the time. This is something that you can be understanding of, but it still is an issue that needs to be managed. By understanding and explaining the context, it is more likely that it will be managed in a way that doesn't further impact on family relationships in a negative way.

In order to work out your identity, you need a sense of who you are and what you are becoming. Social media sites such as Facebook or Instagram give a quick access route to peers and a wider range of people in society who may seem interesting and appealing, but often these sites give a distorted view of the lives people are living. Instagram 'stars' with millions of followers who get hundreds of thousands of likes can seem to young teens to be living 'perfect' lives but really their lives are just perfectly manufactured and edited to give a particular impression to the people who consume their images.

Many popular bloggers or Instagram stars make money from portraying themselves in a certain way. This is about economics and part of that industry is about manipulation. Young people, when starting out on social media, are largely unaware of this and so you have a role to play in the early stages of your child's interaction with social media by bringing this up in their conversations. It is only through parents taking such action and posing questions and presenting ideas for discussion that young people will learn and be challenged to reflect. Having these conversations early in your child's social media journey really matters as young people can be less inclined to listen to what parents have to say once they become embedded in social media culture.

Most young people are not by nature reflective thinkers. Most young people, particularly in today's media world, are in the main consuming data. Therefore, in order to really support your child in developing a good sense of identity you must take responsibility for creating the opportunities for young people to reflect. You can encourage your child to reflect on this issue of manipulation of one's image by introducing the topic during dinnertime, perhaps using an example of someone who is in the public eye a lot, so as not to make it too personal or about your child.

Everyone wants to feel good about themselves, but the constant viewing of streams of data pertaining to other people's lives can have a negative impact on how young people view themselves. Again, it can be in the unconscious mind. They can become obsessed with the need to be identified in a particular way, such as attractive, thin, sexy or muscular. This can impact negatively on young people's beliefs about themselves and their sense of who they are. And this in turn can trigger anxiety, eating disorders, low mood or narcissistic tendencies.

MIND DEVELOPMENT AND EMOTION

What Is Happening with Adolescents' Emotions?

Adolescence can be a time when many questions arise because of the 'identity formation' task. The intensity of feelings can also be heightened by hormonal changes taking place. It can be hard to face into difficult feelings at any stage, and for adolescents this intensity of feeling can be a new experience. It can be difficult for young people to understand fully what they are feeling and why, and that can lead them to become overwhelmed. As a parent you can make it easier for your teenager to talk about their feelings by talking about emotions regularly and discussing your own feelings too.

It can be embarrassing or uncomfortable for young people to talk to their parents about things that are going on for them on social media. Young people may feel their parents don't understand or relate to their experience, given their different life stage. Therefore, talking to friends or even strangers on social media may feel safer and more comfortable. However, online contact with total strangers is not necessarily safe and there can be a danger of young people being groomed by predators through mainstream social media sites. Because of this, it is important to point out to your child that the people they meet online, particularly those they have never met in person, are not necessarily who they say they are. The Yellow app is an example of such a social media site that has led to child protection experts becoming alarmed about the app being dangerous for young people as by its nature it is attractive to predators. This app, which has become known as 'Tinder for Teens', allows users to upload photos and then hook up with either boys or girls they like the look of by swiping right and having their Snapchat or Instagram handles added to each other. This allows them to then send messages to each other and the app can be used to send explicit sexual content or to meet up for casual sexual encounters. It is a dangerous app and young people need to be warned about the possibility of encountering predatory people online once they are old enough to understand. You need to warn your child of the importance of keeping their settings private and tell them how to ensure their profile is viewable only by people they know. Point out to them that once a photo is uploaded onto social media it is out of their control where that photo ends up.

As many adolescents fear that their parents may react badly in a crisis, it is essential to explicitly tell your child that they can talk to you about absolutely anything without being judged, and then follow through on that in practice. Otherwise, the danger is that your child will seek emotional support elsewhere or they could make the choice to keep their problems hidden and not talk to anyone.

Group Apps and Emotional Issues

Group apps such as Snapchat or WhatsApp do not help a young person if they are dealing with difficult emotions, but when compared to other popular social media apps such as Facebook or Instagram group apps can be perceived as a more supportive environment. This is because conversation happens with one or many friends and the feedback given is not in the form of 'likes'.

Because it does not use 'likes' as a method of responding to what someone shares, young people tend to share a more 'real' sense of what is going on in their life. But while the peer contact for young people in group apps can tend to be more 'real' and less manufactured, it can still be hard to express vulnerability in these online group situations. If your child downloads a group app such as Snapchat, WhatsApp or Viber, talk to them about the possibility of interacting with their friends online but not necessarily feeling good inside. Remind them to always be aware of the fact that people, including themselves, can seem to be one way online but can be feeling something else completely. Ensure that they know what to do if they aren't feeling good about something and they did not want to share this with a group of people. Talk through their options, such as talking to you as their parent or talking to one close friend about what is on their mind. Being social in an online group if they are not feeling good might distract them from how they are feeling, but that doesn't normally make the feeling go away; it just pushes it to the side for a while. While group chats can be fun, sometimes the experience in a group chat can be difficult too. A person can be hiding feelings from friends or even from themselves as they engage in group chats or they can feel left out. It is useful to acknowledge this fact, and to tell your child that if they ever find themselves in this situation that it is ok to share any feelings they may have with you.

How Can You Protect Your Child from What They See Online?

Making children and young people aware of their own level of mind development is a good way to prepare them to mind themselves, both physically and emotionally, online. In this sense, knowledge gives some power to the young person to keep themselves safe.

Filters are important but they will not be enough to protect young people from seeing images or coming across content that they may find upsetting. As a basic step, you need to stay clued in to what your child is engaging with online. This means knowing what apps they are using, who they are following, their reasons why, etc. It is good to show an interest and stay involved, rather than just take on a monitoring or supervisory role. One option is to know your child's passwords, but how you use them can be negotiated as your child grows. For example, when your child sets up a social media profile initially you can regularly check what they are saying and doing online, as they are only beginning to learn how to manage this new environment. They will need support and guidance, not just so that they stay safe, but to ensure they don't cause harm to anyone else with their posts and comments too. Seeking permission before posting someone else's image is an example of the type of lesson that needs to be taught early on and this initial period of regularly checking your child's device can be an opportunity to check in with them regarding such issues.

As time goes on and as, perhaps, your child's online and offline relationships develop and deepen, they will desire more privacy and this checking in on posts – in a mentoring rather than supervisory way – can be negotiated again. Your child may want a deeper level of privacy than you are comfortable with. Whatever agreement is reached, it is important that you still know their passwords. This will, at the very least, cause your child to pause and think before they post or send something. Again, the issue of secure attachment comes into play here. If you have a secure attachment with your child, which is about the quality of the bond between you, it is highly unlikely that your child will seek to keep a second social media profile, separate to the one that you as parent can see. How to develop and then maintain a secure attachment bond is explored in detail in Chapter 3. It is also necessary not to be too controlling or too over-involved in your child's life. Once there is an openness in your relationship with your child, an ability to hear them when they speak about their desire for some privacy, there should be no need for them to keep secret profiles. Trust is a massive issue, including your child's trust in you that you have their best interests at heart.

Another way to protect your child is to equip them early, before adolescence even begins, with awareness as to the potential impact of what they view on how they think of themselves or the world. One example might be how women are often portrayed in the media in a particularly sexualised way. Viewing images of women deemed to be the 'correct' or 'desirable' body shape can create difficulties for both boys and girls. Young boys can begin to fall into the trap of thinking that they need to assess people on the basis of their physical attributes while young girls can begin to feel lower self-worth if their physical attributes are not in line with what's fashionable. Young boys can be affected too if their self-worth becomes tied to appearance. It is true that young people, by and large, all want to look well, but with the selfie culture now so much a part of online life conversations about body image, before ever a child joins social media, are necessary. As the identity formation task is happening in the unconscious mind, young people are largely unaware of its impact.

As time goes on, you can tune into whether or not your child is internalising negative ideas about themselves based on what they are seeing online. If this occurs and is not spoken about, it can increase the risk of your child being negatively impacted by such images going forward. You can take protective action by starting a conversation with your child about how various images make them feel. Encourage them to express their feelings and show an interest and curiosity about what they say. Young people deserve to feel good about themselves so you need to allow them space to feel heard, rather than coming up with the best ideas and imposing them as 'truth'. Regularly asking your child how they got on online and whether anything they saw that impacted on their own sense of who they are gives insight into the content they are consuming, but also prompts them to reflect.

THE DIFFERENCE BETWEEN HOW ADOLESCENTS AND ADULTS THINK

During adolescence young people start the journey from concrete to abstract thinking. This means that young people of age ten, eleven or twelve are only starting to move towards, and are not yet fully able to think in complex ways. Throughout adolescence, part of the mind development involves this journey from black-and-white (concrete) thinking to complex (abstract) thinking. And, like all people on any journey, it takes a different length of time for each person to reach the end destination.

As a child, things can seem fairly straightforward. For children, thinking is 'concrete' (or black and white). Children have a definite view of things, and see things in a simplistic way. They see, for example, people as good or bad, as nice or not nice. As children become adolescents, their minds start to develop a capacity for abstract thinking. For some this happens in early adolescence. For others, it starts much later on. It is important to tune into where your child is on this journey from concrete to abstract thinking. So for example, if someone treats them less than ideally online, are they able to see that maybe this friend was just having a bad day, or maybe they were jealous and that is why they posted a mean comment, or maybe they were angry and posted a comment without thinking it through first? If your child is able to see these possibilities, with your support, then it is suggestive of them being some way towards abstract thinking. If, however, they are very black and white about it and don't want to be friends with this person because of that one comment, then it could be that they are being quite concrete in their thinking and they need some support from you to look at whether that is serving them well. If you support them to see it from three different angles, they might still decide to cut contact with this friend who posted the mean comment, but at least they are giving themselves options in how they respond and feel, if they can think about it in a more abstract way. Also, if your child is following anyone online who has very radical views, it could be that concrete thinking is a factor in them becoming radicalised. Again, it helps if you talk to your child about the potential risk of taking anyone's view as gospel truth. It helps for them to have knowledge about the value of abstract thinking. Understanding this journey of change can reduce parent–child conflict throughout adolescence, particularly during those moments when the young person seems to be digging their heels in. For example, if your child seems to be refusing to acknowledge your point of view when it comes to rules about curfews, it could just be that they haven't the capacity to see things from anyone else's point of view because they are thinking in a very concrete way.

What Is Abstract Thinking?

Abstract thinking is a way of thinking that is characterised by the ability to use concepts and to understand generalisations. So, for example, the idea that someone could treat many people well but is mean to a few could be understood by an abstract thinker but not really by a concrete thinker. A concrete thinker would not be able to understand how a person could be both kind and unkind. An abstract thinker would be better able to grasp this concept and wouldn't necessarily need to think of a particular person to gain an understanding of it as they can understand the idea as a concept.

The ability to think in an abstract way means that you can see things differently than you could before. Things can be viewed from a number of different perspectives, which means they can be understood in more complex ways. But abstract thinking develops over time rather than automatically when you reach the age of thirteen. And getting to age eighteen does not mean you have developed a full capacity to think in this abstract way. Some people never manage to fully engage abstract thinking and remain quite concrete in their thinking all of their adult lives.

How Does Thinking in a Concrete or Abstract Way Affect Adolescents?

Everyone develops differently and everyone's journey is unique. Understanding the way cognitive development happens and having an awareness of your own child's stage of cognitive development is a useful thing to focus some attention on, as the way young people think impacts so much on how they feel, what behaviour they engage in, and how they interpret and understand what others may say and do to them. Having a conversation with your child about the difference between concrete and abstract thinking and then asking them how they feel that journey is going for them is a great way to increase their awareness and put it into focus for them. One way to do this would be to ask their view on some latest trend that they seem interested in online. If it is something that people are spending money on, for example makeup, it can be good to introduce the idea of the economics behind social media marketing, just so your child begins to see that there is more to any story than 'This is trendy so I need to have it.' Explaining to a young person that their concrete thinking can leave them gullible to buying something just because it's trendy can put the young person in a more powerful position regarding how they invest their time and money. Marketeers know how young people think and so it's good for young people to be supported to see the wider context.

It is important to be aware that young people are transitioning and moving between the two ways of thinking; at times young people can be very concrete, for example, when they have a point to make or when they hold a position fiercely, perhaps a point of view relating to a peer. This can in part relate to the identity formation task, which leads to the young person taking a definite position in order to work out what position fits. At other times, for example if a parent is discussing how it is possible for someone who seems so nice and friendly to have an ulterior motive, young people can show the capacity to think in an abstract way if they are supported to do so.

Young people are not being intentionally argumentative when they don't see things from a parent's point of view. When you take into consideration their developmental task, which can result in distancing from parents, as well as their journey away from concrete thinking, it is clear that young people are grappling with a lot. It can be the case that their point of view relates more to their developmental stage and their method of thinking rather than to them being oppositional. Understanding this can take the heat out of disagreements. This context sets the scene for the parent to be in a better position to support the young person and understand them, which in turn sets the scene for young people to better understand themselves.

Where Does Abstract Thinking Fit into Identity Development?

There are five main aspects involved in forming an identity during adolescence, of which abstract thinking is one. The five aspects are:

- Developing abstract thinking
- Developing more complex ideas about human relationships and how relationships are
- Identifying personal moral standards
- Understanding and developing an ability to express complicated emotional experiences
- Forming friendships that are mutually close and supportive

While young people cannot see inside their own mind, it can be very useful for them to know something about their own stage of mind development. Their mind task of identity formation and their move from concrete to abstract thinking are concepts that most adolescents can readily understand when it is explained to them. As a parent, you can instigate a conversation about what may be going on in their mind, based on this knowledge. You can share information about where, in terms of mind development, your child may be at. You can then ask your child what they think about these concepts.

When your child is on social media it can be useful to open up a conversation about the idea of a personal moral code. This kind of conversation makes space for your child to reflect on and work out their own ideas about right and wrong. Topics like friendships, strong emotions and how emotions get expressed can all usefully be brought into everyday conversation. Having a warm relationship where communication happens regularly makes it more possible for these specific conversations to take place. And this warmth also makes it possible to talk openly about the great things social media has to offer. Opportunities to follow mental health blogs, musicians and human rights organisations, for example, can all be discussed with your child. Many young people find their way to people and sites of interest to them anyway but by introducing the conversation about what it is they are drawn to or what they think of a certain blog can help steer young people in a direction that is safe and also extremely gratifying.

IDENTITY FORMATION AND SEX

Identity formation during adolescence includes sexual identity. So for young people, how they portray themselves online will feed into how they believe others see them as sexual people and this then feeds into their own developing sense of themselves as a sexual being.

The development of adolescent sexuality is complex as many changes are taking place at a physical and biological level as well as at a psychological and emotional level. All this change is a lot for young teens to be grappling with. Puberty, which brings physical change, also results in increased sexual feelings. This can increase dramatically a young person's interest in and curiosity about sex, and young people from the age of twelve or thirteen years (or very often younger children) begin to show more interest in topics of a sexual nature. Therefore, you need to be aware of the potential role of social media in becoming the go-to place for your child to explore and express sexual curiosity and in influencing their ideas about themselves as a sexual being.

Ready access to sexualised images and porn, as well as personally made porn such as sexual images (sexts) and homemade videos with sexual content, causes difficulty for parents when it comes to keeping their children safe. It can be hard for teens to resist looking for porn or coming across it accidentally, and even if their own phone has a filter and they cannot access porn on their own device they may see it on someone else's phone. Rather than burying your head in the sand or taking a very 'preachy' tone and ordering your child not to view it, you can take on the role of supporting and mentoring your child to manage this highly sexualised environment. In terms of talking to young people about pornography, you should begin these conversations before your child goes on social media sites at all. When talking to your child about porn, keep the following points in mind:

- View talking about porn as an extension of talking about sex.
- Be upfront and acknowledge that your child may be curious about sexual images or may at some point be asked to send a sexual image of themselves.
- Be clear that porn is not real, it is manufactured and it is a performance. Explain that as young people see porn before they are old enough to experience a sexual relationship their ideas about sexual relationships can become unrealistic.

- Explain that the bodies of the people in the porn are not even real bodies much of the time as they are often digitally manipulated or cosmetically enhanced and so comparing their bodies to those they see in porn creates unrealistic expectations. (An example of this is the upsurge in young girls feeling the need to get rid of all pubic hair as this is what is seen in porn and girls feel boys will expect that they too have no pubic hair.)
- Explain that porn frequently portrays people as sexual objects and minimises or neglects the important issue of consent. Therefore, young people who watch porn, before having had experience of real sexual relationships, can begin to objectify other people. This can result in them finding it harder to chat to or relate to others in a real, face-to-face way if they find the person sexually attractive and so, if engaging with the other person sexually, they can forget to seek consent as they see them as an object.

Young people deserve to have this information and it is part of what will keep them safe. Studies have found that young people who access sexual content online are more likely to begin sexual relationships at a young age and to engage in risky sexual practices. And while it is normal for young people to have an interest in and a curiosity about the viewing of sexual content, it is important to be open with your children about the dangers of accessing sexualised content online. By not talking about it, you can unintentionally give the message that porn is harmless. Before they can emotionally cope with intimacy, young people can receive messages from the sexual content they view that tells them that sex is a purely physical act, and so unless you talk to them about it your child can be unprepared for the emotional impact of sex. As part of your discussion on porn, you can warn your child that viewing pornography can become addictive and can also impact on and disrupt their future sexual lives and their ability to form intimate and fulfilling bonds.

Most young people are uncomfortable talking to parents about sexual matters, but by acknowledging that sexual development is taking place and that sex is a natural part of life you can encourage your child to talk and to recognise the artificiality and dangers of porn.

Sex and Social Media

There are four main risks to young people online when it comes to sex and their sexual identity:

- They can become self-loathing because they do not live up to their idea of what it is to be 'sexy' and therefore 'of worth'.
- They can become obsessed with their looks and somewhat narcissistic as a result, and they continuously need to present themselves in a sexual way to others in order to feel of worth.
- They can become addicted to pornography and this becomes a hidden part of their life.
- They can fall into the trap of being 'groomed' by sexual predators or people taking advantage of them as they like the feeling of being deemed 'desirable' and therefore of worth.

A lot goes on for teenagers below the surface. In order to keep them safe online, you need to be aware of these risks and bring what is underneath to the surface. To begin to look below the surface at what goes on, you can introduce some words for discussion with your teen. While the basics of sex and porn should be your starting point, terms such as *sexualisation* and *consent* will give your child a greater understanding of how to manage sexual issues on social media. And that in turn will help keep them and others they interact with safe.

To *sexualise* means to make something sexual in quality. So for example, to photograph a person's body with the camera pointing at and emphasising the parts of the body that might sexually stimulate. It is not necessarily done with the person's consent, for example images of celebrities that appear online are often taken without consent. People can sexualise themselves too, both boys and girls, and sometimes people do it without knowing that what they are doing is sexualising themselves and therefore objectifying themselves to a certain degree. An example would be a profile picture for a social media site that emphasises the sexual nature of the person in the photograph. Often this objectifying of the self is done in order to be deemed attractive and sexual to others, which is fine and part of life. But it is dangerous too, particularly for young people who are not yet clear on their own emerging sexual identity. By focusing on their own sexual attractiveness and how to package and frame their sexual 'parts' online in order to sexually attract others, young people can begin to see themselves as objects. And that can place them at risk of being treated like an object, which is dangerous when it comes to the issue of consent.

Consent is the agreement a person gives for something to happen. It is important that young people are clear about consent when it comes to social media for a number of reasons. One is that consent is needed to share someone else's images or content. If a person posts something publicly, for everyone to see, it can be assumed that consent to share the image/content has been given. But it's not good to assume and it's worth talking to your child about how it is not ok to ever upload anyone else's information or image onto social media without their consent. If you don't explicitly tell your child this they won't be aware of it and they also won't know that it is ok for them to say 'no' to others who wish to put their information or image up online. On an app such as Snapchat, where images are sent and often only last a few seconds, what happens if an image is sent to someone and a screenshot of that image is saved? Who then owns the image? Pose this question to your child before they use Snapchat. Ensure that they know that the image belongs to the person who took it and consent needs to be requested and received clearly before they can share it.

When it comes to porn, the risk around objectification has already been outlined and so it is vital that young people are informed clearly at home that consent is absolutely essential before any sexual contact can happen between them and other people. In discussing the issue of consent, you need to make space to talk about the different ways that consent can be talked about during a sexual encounter. For example, young people may find the question 'Are you ok to have sex with me?' too direct to ask someone they are with and so they will need to think ahead of time of what else they could say in a situation. And what if the encounter is with more than one person at a time? Even checking if someone is feeling ok about what is going on can be a way into a conversation about consent. If you say 'Are you ok with what we are doing?' or even 'Are you ok right now?' it will be pretty clear to the person on the receiving end of that comment that the person asking the question does not see them as an object. Make sure your child has language to communicate about consent.

Within the world of social media, it is hard not to be exposed to the process of sexualisation, particularly for young women. Teens today are growing up in an environment where numerous messages are being sent to them covertly, and often overtly, on a daily basis through advertisements, music videos, magazines and online content. At no time in our world before have young people been so bombarded with 'celebrity' culture and ideas about what is deemed to be 'sexually attractive' and therefore of worth. Adults too are bombarded with sexualised content and images but they have the benefit of being able to think in an abstract way about such content and, as adults are not dealing with the task of identity formation, many of these images can seem to have little or no impact on us at all. But the sexualisation does impact young people as they are at an age where they are trying to work out how the world works. They are also trying to work out how to fit into it. Young people still think in quite a concrete way and so if they don't feel attractive or worthy of attention it can impact their mental health, self-esteem and their ability to form close bonds.

As well as being concrete thinkers, young people have not yet had the chance to fully develop their own moral code. So while you can say that something is right or wrong this reflects your own moral code, and your child may move away from that position as part of their identity formation process. Therefore starting a discussion with a definition is a good concrete way to introduce the topic of sexuality and sex online. This makes it about the issue, rather than focusing on your ideas and theirs about right and wrong. Having discussed the definitions, you can then use an example of someone, perhaps a celebrity, who portrays themselves in a certain way. Ask your child if that person has been sexualised. If the answer is yes, then have they been sexualised by others? By themselves? By both others and themselves? Through this discussion your child becomes aware of sexualisation as a process. This gives them the power then to decide how they wish to engage (or not) with this process online:

- Do they want to sexualise themselves?
- Why? Is it to be liked?
- Do they wish for others to sexualise them?
- What might this do to their ability to relate to others in relationships with them?
- What might it do to their own sense of their worth?

It is risky to link your sense of yourself as a sexualised person too much to confidence. The confidence is not only coming from a narrow source, but the source is external. That means you cannot really control it. This issue will be addressed more in Chapter 2. And while each young person gets to make up their own mind about where they stand on the issue of sexualisation, it is very much an issue of our time. Knowing these definitions gives young people information, which gives them power. By bringing them into conversation you are bringing them into consciousness. It is one of the steps towards keeping young people safe online.

2

STEP TWO: UNDERSTANDING CONFIDENCE AND ITS SOURCES

'Be who you are and say what you feel, because those who mind don't matter and those who matter don't mind.'

Bernard Baruch, American financier and
political consultant, 1870–1965

THE CONTEXT OF CONFIDENCE

Growing up in today's world, your child will have an expectation that they will be on social media and it will be a part of their world. And sometimes this desire is being met at a young age. Children as young as nine or ten are allowed access social media sites; some have smart phones at this age. And while supervised internet use for the purpose of playing games, completing homework or listening to music is safe for children, connecting socially online is a task that is too complex, socially and psychologically, for young children to manage well. Part of the reason is that the experience of connecting online can very quickly become a source of confidence and that's not good at all. To source too much confidence from the number of contacts you have or the number of likes you get on an Instagram post is unhealthy as the child can become reliant on a certain number of likes, contacts or followers to feel good. The more connections a child has, the more they can begin to believe that they are doing something right and it can become a bit of an obsession.

Confidence is relevant when it comes to social media because it relates closely to self-esteem. If your child begins to develop a relationship with social media that results in them sourcing their confidence outside of themselves it is extremely risky. That is true whether they have a high level of confidence or not. To need validation from others in order to feel confident is a perilous place for young people to be. We all need to be able to feel good about ourselves despite what others may say to us or about us. And for young people, the fact that they are still working out their identity and therefore are highly sensitive to feedback makes them more vulnerable. A positive sense of their own worth is the root of a positive, healthy self-image for your child.

Before your child establishes a social media profile it is important for them to know that there are two main sources of confidence: an external source, such as feedback from others about themselves, and an internal source, which can be the thoughts they have about themselves, the little voice in their head that hopefully whispers, 'Go you, well done to me there.' While most people get confidence from both sources, the internal source is much healthier than the external as you can gain control of it. If your child is not aware of this – if they are not encouraged to tune into their internal confidence source and build up their control of this source – they could fall into the trap quite quickly of using social media itself as a confidence source.

The Impact of the Industry v Inferiority Task on Confidence

If your child has yet to reach adolescence, they are dealing with the 'Industry v Inferiority' task. This is the task faced between the ages of approximately five and twelve or thirteen. If your child is that age, they are trying, at an unconscious level, to figure out if they can make it and accomplish 'doing the right thing' in their world. And so if they feel that they can accomplish things – follow social rules, get along with other children in the yard and outside of school – they are likely to begin adolescence feeling that yes, they are able to 'make it' and work out how to navigate within the world. This is good for their confidence. Having access to social media while this psychological task is still being worked out can complicate your child's experience of social relationships. They won't be getting the chance to think through how others may respond to what they say or do online in the way they would if they were in the yard as the social interaction is less direct. They would also be missing the important context of body language and tone of voice to help interpret others' behaviour. If your child is a pre-teen, they are at a less advanced stage of development and so they have less ability to empathise. Therefore, they are less able to think ahead about how their words and actions online might impact on another child. It is important for you as a parent to tune into how accessing social media at a young age could impact on:

- Your child's confidence (you don't want their confidence source to suddenly transfer to feedback from social media)
- How your child is thinking about and treating others (your child needs the opportunity to develop awareness about how something that is exciting and funny for them to post may be experienced by a friend as hurtful and upsetting)

Just because your child is tech-savvy does not mean they are ready for socialising online. They probably are not aware of how much confidence they have or how they are sourcing confidence and that's a risk because being aware of how much confidence they have is like knowing what strength of protection they have. Feelings such as anxiety or depression are common for young people online whose confidence gets knocked. And engaging in behaviours which are sexually risky or self-harming can be triggered by problems with confidence. Confidence is essential for young people online and you are in a prime position to support your child to develop a healthy source of confidence that will keep them safe and well.

Confidence is acquired to varying degrees as each person goes through the experience of living their life. As a young child, regularly receiving praise and encouragement can provide the foundation for a solid sense of their own worth and this feedback can be the main source of confidence for a young child. Excelling at sport or school-work and being popular with peers can become important sources of confidence for a child too. But these sources are still external and if the child becomes too dependent on any one of these external sources problems can begin (for example, a child who sources most of their confidence from being one of the smartest in their class can feel insecure and anxious if they don't do well in a test). As adolescence approaches, and your child moves into the next stage of mind development (identity formation), they will inevitably start to look more to the external world in order to get feedback about themselves. It is essential therefore that your child knows both the value of reflecting on their confidence sources and how to do it.

How to Reflect on Your Confidence

How young people value themselves affects not just how they interact with others socially but also how they think about themselves. So it is vital for young people to reflect and gain awareness of what their inner voice tends to say to them about themselves. Whether they deem themselves to be worthy of love, respect or ridicule impacts on how events are interpreted as well as how they behave and react in various situations. A young person who believes they deserve respect will be more likely to call someone out for being mean online, but if they think they deserve ridicule they most likely won't stand up for themselves. Reflecting on thoughts about themselves and their confidence is not something young people naturally tend to do. Therefore you need to step in and take the lead. Begin by talking quite generally about confidence and where it comes from, and mentioning your own confidence sources and where you think your own level of confidence is at. The issue of confidence and how it is sourced needs to be discussed openly and regularly with young people. This discussion will move the issue of confidence sources up into their conscious mind, which is necessary if young people are to develop resilience to mental health difficulties as they go online.

You can support your child to reflect on confidence firstly by bringing up in conversation how important confidence is, particularly when online. By being very clear that there are different types of confidence and by explaining what this means, you are giving your child the opportunity to increase their awareness. You can explain that confidence is one of the most important tools they need online in order to stay happy and well. When you have introduced the topic of confidence and have told your child how important their confidence is as 'armour' for them online, you can go on to ask the following questions. The questions do not need a definite answer; they are just to facilitate discussion. Asking the question and exploring the ideas will prompt your child to reflect.

- What does confidence mean to me?
- Do I know I am worthy of love and respect?
- What do these words – love and respect – mean (to me)?
- How do/how can others show love and respect to me?
- How do I show it to others?
- What do I expect from others when it comes to treating me with respect?
- What do I expect from myself?
- Does it matter to me that I am respected/that I feel respected?
- Do I learn from those around me that love and respect matters?
- Do I act in a way towards myself that is loving and respectful of me?

Explaining Sources of Confidence to Your Child

Once your child has started to reflect even a little bit about how they feel about themselves, you can introduce the idea of confidence sources. The place your child's confidence comes from is their confidence source. Confidence has two main sources: inside the self or outside of the self. Confidence coming from outside of the self (feedback from others) is not as reliable as the internal source (feedback from yourself) and that is why it is best to rely on the internal source as it is sustainable. (For it to become sustainable involves gaining a good level of control over your thoughts. This is covered in Chapter 4.) For very young children, who have not yet developed control over their thoughts, getting confidence through feedback from others like parents is crucial to their developing self-esteem. Young children are not yet able to fully manage being able to think in a way that impacts positively on their own confidence, but by age ten or eleven your child will grasp the concepts.

Once your child is approaching an age where you feel they are nearly ready to use social media, they need to know how to start minding their own confidence and sourcing it inside themselves to a greater extent. If they don't learn to do this, it could mean that they end up needing feedback from social media in order to feel validated and confident. This then can create risk. One of the main issues with social media is that the confidence young people get from it is external. Needing constant feedback from others in order to feel good about yourself is not good for mental health. When you think of the environment of social media, the feedback given on social media can often be very direct in the form of definite 'likes' or positive comments, or it can be indirect. But whether it is explicit or subtle, direct or indirect, this feedback is external and cannot be relied upon. And even if it was considered reliable for a particular individual (for example, a physically attractive girl who always gets 'likes' for her selfies) it can be very detrimental to a person's overall well-being to become fixated on a very narrow aspect of themselves in order to source confidence. For some young people, getting likes on Facebook or Instagram posts can consume vast amounts of time and dictate hugely what they think about. Social media is a very narrow filter through which to determine a person's worth and your child needs to be told that before ever they socialise online. Many young people are unknowingly letting social media feedback define their worth to a large extent. Some spend vast amounts of time and energy editing selfies and manipulating their body image in order to get 'likes' and look like celebrities. It is detrimental to mental health and it has become ubiquitous, as any scroll through adolescent profile pictures will confirm. Internal confidence is key to good mental health and even if young people continue to source their confidence externally, at least having knowledge about the importance of having two confidence sources gives them a choice.

In order to be psychologically safe and mentally well, and in order to be successful in achieving their goals and asserting their wishes, it is useful for young people to be aware of how much self-confidence they possess. Without self-confidence a person will live in a constant pool of self-doubt. They can develop anxiety and/or depression and these are difficult issues for any young person to have to deal with. Low self-confidence places young people at potential risk of doing something they are not that comfortable doing online, in order to stay in with the crowd or to impress someone. And while confidence varies in different types of situations (for example, more confidence at home than in school or more confidence in one-to-one social situations than in a large group), it is true that most people have a level of confidence that is normal for them. So on a scale of 1 to 10, if 1 was having hardly any confidence and 10 was being full of confidence, most people would 'normally' be around 2, or 5 or 8. This level is what they experience as their confidence level most of the time and is therefore their 'norm.' If you ask your child where on this scale they believe their confidence to be, they become more aware of their confidence level and then will notice if it starts to go up or down.

THE CONFIDENCE CIRCLE

A confidence circle is a tool that allows the person using it to work out where their confidence is coming from and how much confidence they have. People, generally speaking – and this includes adults as well as young people – do not pay attention to where their confidence comes from and so, when they lose it, it can be hard to get it back. In my clinical experience, using the confidence circle is a simple technique that really works with young people who have lost confidence. And as a technique, it can be used as a way to gain awareness of confidence sources and learn how to ensure that confidence is not coming too much from one source.

To help your child create their own confidence circle draw a circle and assign a slice of the circle to each confidence source. This could include a talent, an aspect of yourself or your personality, feedback from others, and so on. Here's an example of one child's confidence circle:

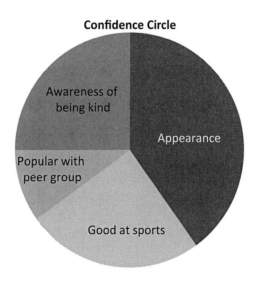

Confidence Circle

Awareness of being kind

Appearance

Popular with peer group

Good at sports

- 40% comes from appearance
- 25% comes from being good at sport
- 10% comes from being popular with their peer group

That leaves a gap of 25% which could, with reflection, start to come from an internal source such as awareness of themselves as being kind. Young people who find it very difficult to fill in the circle (and many young people would find it hard to fill it all in) are indicating one of two things:

- A very low level of confidence or
- A lack of awareness about confidence

Both of these scenarios, if discovered, can be resolved.

Why Do Young People Need to Pay Attention to Their Confidence Source?

The source of your child's confidence can change and sometimes this can happen without them even realising it. It can happen suddenly or gradually over time, depending on the circumstances of their life, what they are doing, how they are being treated and what they are thinking. On social media, young people are very exposed to what others think of them and the feedback others give them. Young people post comments quickly without really thinking through the consequences for the person on the receiving end and so it is important for your child to be aware of how this feedback alters their confidence. Confidence can fluctuate wildly for some young people on social media. They can feel elated and full of confidence one minute, deflated and down the next, and that fluctuation indicates that too much of their confidence is being sourced from an external place.

For confidence to become more stable, it is essential that the internal source of confidence is activated. This means your child needs to tune into their thoughts about themselves and ensure that these thoughts are not self-critical. Whether your child's source of confidence is mostly external or mostly internal is a choice they can make for themselves only if they know it is a choice that they can make. No one can control where your child sources their confidence except for them. But you need to tell them they have a choice.

Here's an exercise you can ask your child to complete before they are allowed on social media: draw a circle and think about slicing it as you would a cake, each slice representing how much an aspect of their life gives them confidence. Take the opportunity to suggest positive attributes to them that do not readily come to their own mind. By doing this, you can influence what can become an internal confidence source. For example, being kind or loving towards a sibling or loyal towards a friend can be something that is obvious to you as a parent but it may not be something your child is aware of unless it is pointed out. If you have the opportunity to have these conversations with your child before they are on social media at all the benefit will be greater. That is because children of a younger age are not yet dealing with the task of identity formation. Therefore, they are less likely to be disagree with what you are saying about them and they will be more likely to take on board the positive things you say. Once adolescence begins, it is the beginning of your child tending to listen to peers more and you that bit less. If your child cannot fill in the circle and can only think of one thing that gives them confidence (being good at sport, for example), it is worth spending time focusing on how to increase their internal confidence. You can ask other people in the family what they imagine might give this particular child confidence. Even though this invites external responses and therefore is an externally sourced piece of confidence, it can lead to the young person internalising something that is said by a family member about them, for example, 'They are always helpful' or 'They have a great sense of humour'. By being encouraged to own these positive aspects of themselves, they will be able to develop their internal confidence source.

For example, Michael's mother says to his father, in front of Michael, 'Michael and I have been talking about where he gets his confidence from and it was hard for him to think of anything other than being good at sport that made him feel confident and good about himself. Can you think of any other sources of confidence for Michael?' Michael's father says, 'I always see Michael making an effort and I really admire that trait.' Michael can then take this external source, 'My dad believes I make an effort and that makes me feel confident' and translate it into an internal source of confidence: 'I am now aware of how much effort I make and how important that is so it is something going forward that can be a source of confidence.'

The fact that a child can gain awareness about and then internalise a positive aspect of themselves is important. It means that making an effort and feeling confident about their own ability to do that will start to matter. Once it matters to them, it can be a source of confidence for them, even when no one is around to witness it and give them praise for it. Internalising positive feedback about an aspect of themselves is important for children as they grow. Starting a conversation about internal confidence is a way to make this internalising more likely to happen for your child.

It is up to each person to decide whether or not the ways they get confidence work well for them. You can guide your child through this and even if they are an adolescent they are still open to being influenced by what you say you believe. Generally speaking, it is better to have many sources of confidence so that if one source goes, your confidence does not drop completely. To explain this to your child, you can use the example of a football star and ask them what they think would happen to that footballer if they suddenly couldn't play football anymore because they were dropped from the team or were injured. If being good at football is the only thing in the world that makes them feel good about themselves it is likely that they will be at risk of losing an awful lot of confidence, which can then lead to low mood, anxiety, depression or withdrawal from others. Another example could be a reality star who gets all of their confidence from the fact that they are famous and on the cover of magazines. If this person suddenly becomes unpopular or isn't on the cover of magazines any more their self-esteem can take a massive hit if it was the main thing that made them feel good about themselves. These are examples that even children as young as nine or ten can understand. You need to not rely on one aspect of your life to feel confident. It is risky to your self-esteem and mental health if you do.

At different times, confidence goes up and confidence goes down. But being aware of the slices of the circle or the sources of confidence helps in situations where confidence tends to dip. So while each 'slice' of the circle represents a source of confidence, it is important to ask about how confident the young person feels in different situations. Then suggest that giving some thought to these 'slices' before going into a situation that might threaten confidence in some way – for example, entering a room with a large crowd – is a way to keep confidence levels steady.

If it is difficult for your child to fill in the circle, ask if it is because it is hard to reflect and think about what gives them confidence or if it is that they feel their confidence is very low. If it is a difficulty with reflecting, spend some time encouraging your child to reflect on something that isn't about them, such as the latest game or trend or some piece of music they have listened to. Questions such as 'Why do you think you tend to like that type of music?' and 'What do you think people like about that trend?' facilitates a move towards reflective thinking. If their difficulty with filling in the confidence circle is due to low confidence generally and your child cannot think of anything that gives them confidence, it is fortunate that you found that out before they began using social media and you can now work with them to help increase their confidence levels, perhaps by helping them make sure they are not being self-critical in their thoughts about themselves. This is discussed in the next section on perceptions.

THE POWER OF PERCEPTION

What Does Perception Really Mean?

Our perceptions are how we see and understand what is happening in our environment. Others' perceptions of us are how others understand us to be. Young people tune into how others perceive them to be. In society and on social media (as social media reflects the ideas in society) young people are exposed to ideas about what is perceived to be 'of worth'. Because these ideas are dominant and all around us they take on the status of being true, even though they are just beliefs. An example of this is how we are bombarded with images and content of people (some famous) who are deemed to be of high worth simply because of how they present themselves to be physically. And when this idea is broken down, the message that it feeds your child is that how you look is the most important aspect of who you are as a person. This idea is dominant, particularly in teenage and celebrity culture. You need to not only be aware of your own position in relation to this idea (do you agree with it or not) but you also need to be tuning in to what ideas your child is developing about this 'truth'.

Social media is a vehicle through which many young people start to work out their identity and this ties into their sense of worth. As young people place so much value on other people's opinions of how they are, or others' perceptions, you need to be aware that this carries risk. If a situation arises where your child, whether they have a high level of externally sourced confidence or low confidence, perceives another person to not think highly of them their confidence can drop drastically and suddenly. Impulsively engaging in self-harm is one of the possible consequences of a sudden feeling of despair. Teenagers can engage in this behaviour to escape the pain of feeling worthless. Another danger is that they can get into a risky situation that they did not plan on getting into, for example, sexting, even though they are not comfortable doing so, just to give someone the impression that they are 'of worth'. You can helpfully ask questions such as:

- What qualities/attributes do you admire or value in your friends and the celebrities you like?
- What do you think makes a person special?
- What makes you special?
- How much does a person's appearance matter?

These questions give space for your child to reflect on what matters about people. It is likely that for your child, choosing a friend is not a decision they make based completely on how another person looks. And yet, so much effort is spent on looking a certain way for others it's as if it is the thing that matters most. Have regular conversations with your child early on about how one-dimensional it is to just assess someone based on how they look and make sure they know that they should not assess themselves based on how they look either. If you find them to be self-critical in terms of their thinking about themselves, it is important to point out the danger of this. In order to feel good, we all have to learn to love ourselves. Children won't necessarily think about this unless they are encouraged to and it's necessary before they begin to use social media that your child knows how to identify a self-critical thought. The importance of tuning into one's thoughts is explored more in Chapter 4 but in relation to this issue around appearance it is important that we tell our children that they need to practice kindness in how they think about themselves. There is way too much pressure on young people when it comes to appearance. Make sure your child knows that we all look different and we need to love ourselves just the way we are. Give them this mantra to repeat to themselves when necessary: 'We all look different; I love myself just the way I am.' This will help when it comes to them being on social media, where there is so much emphasis placed on appearance.

Young people need to think about how much time they spend wondering or stressing over what others think of them. They also need to work out how they are interpreting things, both the specific words of others and the more indirect feedback they get from the way others act towards them. If they start to tune into this, they will know:

- How much importance they are placing on other people's opinions of them and
- How they are interpreting feedback they get from others

As adults, how we are perceived matters to varying degrees. We are all different and care to a greater or lesser extent about what people think of us. For young people though, they generally are much more tuned in to what others think of them, particularly other people their own age, because of the identity formation task they are undergoing (discussed in Chapter 1). And so they need to perceive things in a way that boosts their confidence rather than in a way that knocks it.

One way for your child to start to understand how much the source of their confidence is external is to ask themselves the following questions:

- What kind of feedback or statements from others impact on how I feel about myself?
- Do I care a lot and pay a lot of attention to what others say about my abilities, appearance, character, achievements?
- Do I have my own ideas about myself that don't depend on what other people think or say about me?

To tune into their confidence levels when they are on social media your child will need to slow down and take the time to focus on how they are feeling by taking breaks from their smart device. You can encourage them to get into the habit of checking on a scale of 1 to 10 where their confidence is at just before they post something on social media. If their confidence is at 1, it is very low; if it's at 9, it's very high. Then, once the post is up, encourage them to check their confidence level again. Has it changed? Are they feeling anxious waiting to see if they get feedback? It is good to scan the body for any anxiety also as that can impact on confidence. Next, they need to tune into how much focus they give to any feedback. If the feedback is in the form of 'likes', how does this affect their confidence on that scale of 1 to 10? Is the anxiety still being felt in their body? What are their thoughts as they check for feedback and count 'likes'? Once they have completed this exercise, you can help them work out how their confidence was affected by asking:

- How confident do you feel?
- How much does it matter to you that your peers liked/did not like the post/selfie?
- Are you surprised that you cared so much/so little?
- Do you want to care so much going forward?

There are no right or wrong ways to feel and it is important that you don't try to impose a way to feel on your child. To tell your child 'You shouldn't care what they think' can be interpreted, especially by a young person going through adolescence, as you trying to tell them what to think. Adolescents can believe that because you are older you do not understand what it is like for them and so it is best if you just enquire about why the feedback matters (if it does) and to focus then on where these thoughts about the feedback being important have come from.

No one can control another person's thoughts and no one but your child can choose what confidence sources to develop. Living in the world as it is today, it is difficult not to be hugely influenced by perceptions others may have developed about how we are all supposed to be. But if your child gets external praise and a confidence boost as a result, whether it is for a selfie posted or amazing exam results, it is important to point out the benefit of balancing this external feedback with internal feedback that comes from the self. Paying attention to how much a particular event or piece of feedback impacts on confidence is crucial for your child's mental well-being. Otherwise, their confidence sources remain outside of their control and that is risky. With selfies being so much a part of the culture today for young people, it is important that they have time to consider and chat with you about what a narrow and shallow filter this is to rate their own or anyone else's worth. Giving your child this message early on makes it more likely that they will build resilience for online life. And they are more likely to take your ideas about this on board if they haven't been on social media yet.

Listening more to peers than parents in order to figure out who they are in the world is the norm and it is good for you to tell your child explicitly that you understand how important contact with their peers is for them as they get older. In conversation about confidence sources, even if your child does not agree with your view, you can clearly state that you don't expect them to. This is the best route to go when discussing confidence sources, rather than trying to tell them how to think. To tell a teenager what they should think or what they should value about themselves could possibly result in them thinking the opposite just so they feel they have space to decide their own mind. Letting them make up their own mind while also keeping regular conversations about confidence going is best.

How Can Young People Develop an Internal Source of Confidence?

One thing is essential in order to develop an internal confidence source and that is awareness of your thoughts. If the thoughts in your child's mind are not encouraging and supportive then this needs attention. Through practice and by monitoring their thoughts anyone can gain better control of their thinking. So, for example, if your child got great exam results and good feedback as a result of that, if they feel good about that, a thought such as 'I did my very best and I am very proud of myself because of that' means that, despite the feedback, their confidence is still being sourced internally.

If they are not aware of how they feel about their own efforts and are thinking (with or without being aware of it), 'I feel great because people think I'm great', the feeling of confidence is at the same level but the source is now external. For the source to become internal, young people need to reflect on what exactly they are thinking, particularly about themselves. They need to:

- Ask themselves what they are thinking and
- Ask whether they want to source the confidence internally and

- If the answer is yes, switch their thought to one that is good about themselves, rather than one based on feedback

You will have many opportunities to bring this process of reflection into everyday conversation. By tuning in to what is happening in your child's day and by asking how an incident or event made them feel or think about themselves you can encourage them to reflect. Broadening the conversation out to look at what their thoughts about themselves are and whether their thoughts are influencing their confidence in a good or bad way is also useful. If the self-thoughts – that little voice that we all tune into in our heads – are having a negative impact on confidence this needs to be challenged.

The first step in challenging negative self-talk is to see the self-critical or negative thought as merely a thought – something that you can hold onto or let go of – and not a fact. Once children realise that they can let go of a thought, they have a choice around it. The younger your child is when they learn about letting go of thoughts the better as they can develop the habit of letting go self-critical thoughts that don't make them feel good. Initially, your child will need support to do this. Pay attention to any negative self-criticism your child may be directing at themselves. Tell them that the self-critical thought is one that doesn't seem to be making them feel good and explain that thoughts are things they can let go of. Ask them to think of an alternative thought (for example, switching 'I'm no good at football' to 'I really love football and sometimes I play well.') Challenging negative self-talk is how a steady internal source of confidence develops. Once this internal source has started to develop, the next thing that young people need to understand is that confidence is like water in a jug.

CONFIDENCE AS A FLUID: THE WATER IN A JUG ANALOGY

A person's level of confidence changes in different situations. It sometimes gets a boost and goes up or it takes a knock and goes down. A person's confidence level may stay the same for quite a while or it may change frequently, depending on different factors. Therefore it is useful to think of confidence as being fluid. Its level changes, just like water in a jug.

Understanding confidence as water in a jug is a simple and effective way for your child to get to know and understand their own confidence as a resource. As confidence is not something that can be seen or touched, it can be hard to really get to know what their confidence is made up of and what can happen to it. That is why comparing it to something tangible that can be visualised works well.

Things happen sometimes that catch young people off guard. Incidents happen or things are interpreted a certain way online, and this can threaten their confidence in some way. The feeling of loss, rejection or hurt can be felt intensely in the context of social media. This can happen if a person feels left out or rejected, or if they are bullied, taunted or exposed in some way. Their confidence can take a sudden knock. When young people start using social media for the first time this is not something they are ready for or expecting to happen to them. Therefore, they are not thinking about how important it is to 'hold their jug steady' so that they do not experience this sudden loss of confidence. They may not even notice their confidence spilling out. Confidence can be lost gradually over time and can reach a very low level without anyone even noticing. If the level of water in the jug (the confidence a person feels in themselves) has dropped suddenly or if the level over time decreases to very low level, it can feel very risky for that person to be sociable at all as any social situation can further impact in a negative way how confident they feel about themselves. If this was to happen to your child, you may start to notice them withdrawing into themselves more. With very low confidence, low self-esteem can develop and your child could start to believe that no one would want to spend time with them. The withdrawal from others happens because unconsciously they may start to believe 'What is the point in me socialising? Nobody would want me around.' This belief can be the mind's way of taking an action which it feels is protective. Imagine the water in the jug again: by withdrawing from real social interaction and perhaps just scrolling through online newsfeeds instead the unconscious mind can be taking your child out of what is deemed to be a psychologically 'risky' situation for them, one in which they could be exposed to further spillage of what little confidence they have left if interactions with others go badly. Often this decision to withdraw is not done consciously; some young people do it gradually and don't even realise it is happening. They are not aware of thinking 'I am going to withdraw from my friends in order to protect the little bit of confidence I have left', but that is in fact what can be happening.

This is why the jug analogy is very helpful. When confidence is critically low we put a cover over the top of our jug to seal it shut. This is an unconscious decision and one that the mind can decide is protective; it can happen to anyone at any age. By sealing the jug shut (withdrawing) no more water (confidence) can be lost, but the danger is that no more water (or confidence) can be gained either. Our confidence level cannot increase. With confidence not increasing, we can become stuck in a place where negative loops of thinking build up in our mind, loops such as 'Why would anyone want to be with me/spend time with me?', leading to 'I am better off staying on my own and away from others.' This can then make it hard to do basic things such as go to school or spend time with friends.

If this type of situation unfolds, the social media world can become appealing as a place to be. But it may be more attractive (and feel safer) to be there as an observer, rather than as an active participant. Young people can be online without actually engaging with others as they feel too threatened psychologically to do so. It can seem safer to interact with strangers or just passively observe content. This can seem to offer a distraction for the young person from difficult emotions that are associated with low confidence, such as anxiety and low mood. But if thinking about themselves has become negative, they can then be at risk of comparing themselves unfavourable to others they view online.

It is important to be aware that for a child with low levels of confidence, being on social media as an observer of others (peers they know or celebrities) can compound negative loops of thinking about themselves. This can further fuel negative self-talk and the young person's own awareness of this happening to them can be low or non-existent. If your child becomes increasingly an observer of others, they can fall into the trap of constantly comparing themselves to others and assessing their worth in a negative and restricted way.

Falling into the habit of viewing pornography in order to source and gain comfort also can come into play at this stage as porn can be an escape that seems to offer comfort. Because viewing pornography demands nothing of the person viewing it, and because sexual arousal makes people feel good, the feeling of low mood that they may be grappling with can be masked. This experience of being comforted by pornography can further exacerbate a young person's difficulties, particularly if the watching of porn becomes something they then depend on in order to feel good.

It is important for your child to understand what can happen to them on an unconscious level if their confidence becomes critically low. If they ever start to unconsciously withdraw from real face-to-face social contact, they need to be able to work out why this has happened. By using the analogy of water in a jug, it is easier for them to understand why someone might withdraw as a protective (and yet self-destructive) step. By explaining this analogy to your child, you are placing them in a more powerful position to tune into their level of confidence on an ongoing basis. If they can talk about their confidence with someone they trust such as you, they can begin to work out ways to increase the level of confidence they have.

If any young person can acknowledge that their level of confidence is critically low, this can be the first piercing of a hole in the cover over the jug. This then is the first small step to allow water (confidence) back in. Expressing or sharing how they feel can be a hard step to take, but once they make one hole in that cover the next won't be as difficult. Gradually confidence can build back up once it has an entry point, and this is true even if confidence has reached a very low level.

CONFIDENCE GETTING KNOCKED

Confidence can get knocked in two ways:

- Something happens that is outside of the young person's control: an external event or something said by someone else
- Negative thinking and negative, self-critical self-talk (which happens inside the self)

If confidence is lost, it is important for your child to tune into what exactly is causing the 'spill' or reduction in the level of confidence, and then to realise the level of control they have over the 'spillage'.

Young people cannot, just as adults cannot, control how others behave or what others may say. Each person can only control their response to what others may say or do. That is where the power lies: in learning to gain control over your mind and how you are interpreting or perceiving things. People say mean things and do mean things for all sorts of reasons on social media, and sometimes the hurt a person feels was not intended. If your child experiences a 'spillage' of confidence triggered by the words or actions of others it is important for them to reflect on how they are interpreting the events that happen in their social media world. For example, if they are excluded by a group of friends on a particular occasion or on a regular basis, perhaps on Snapchat or some other group chat, then your child needs to take action in their mind so that their confidence does not continuously spill out. What action they choose to take is up to them. They may think 'I will ask my friends about this' or 'I am not putting up with this and am going offline for a while.' What matters most is that the action, in terms of conscious thought, is encouraging and supportive of themselves. Thoughts such as 'They mustn't like me' or 'I will try harder to impress them' are unhelpful and damaging as they will further erode confidence.

You need to encourage your child to slow down and pay attention to their interpretation of events. They need to take the space to do this so that they can notice the relationship between their confidence and their thoughts. You can help them with this slowing down by asking how their day went on social media and asking questions such as the following about any incidents that occur:

- How does that make you feel about yourself?
- How are you interpreting that?
- Why do you think that happened?

If a person's confidence is low and they feel excluded their inner voice will say things like 'This hurts so much, they mustn't like me at all.' If their confidence is high and they feel excluded their inner voice is more likely to say 'What's going on here? I'm not putting up with this. I deserve better.' Confidence breeds inner voices that breed confidence. Low confidence is fertile ground for an inner voice that continuously knocks confidence. Encourage your child to tune into their inner voice, which really is just their thoughts. This inner voice can be challenged at any time once the effort is made to do it. The more your child is encouraged to pay attention to their thoughts, the more they can gain control of their mental health and the more they will build the resilience needed for social media.

THE MIND IS A MUSCLE: STRENGTHEN IT

Your child will benefit greatly if they are taught from a young age to think of the mind like a muscle. When the mind is seen in this way it is easier to think about building up strength there. This increased strength of mind will increase their resilience. When young people go online information is being absorbed at a high speed. Therefore they do not have the time to be reflective and do mind-strengthening work. Creating a space for reflecting is very important for young people so that they can develop their own ideas about what it is they value and they think.

By asking some of the following questions, you can prompt your child to reflect on how to hold their jug of water (their confidence) steady when something happens to threaten it:

- Do you feel differently about yourself on different days or is there a general pattern?
- What impact does the way you think about yourself have on your confidence?
- How much do others influence your confidence?
- How confident do you feel to not be affected by any criticism that could come your way?
- Do you feel you could think in a way that holds onto your confidence, if someone was to say something mean to you?

It may seem new and strange for your child to be asked to reflect on their confidence when all they feel about getting access to social media is excited or happy and they don't think of social media as an environment in which they could lose confidence. But giving focus to confidence is an essential step in preparing young people for life online. Without an internal source of confidence, young people become vulnerable. Reflecting on their confidence sources will increase self-awareness and therefore increase their strength of mind.

3

STEP THREE: MAKING ATTACHMENT SECURE

'Relationships are the most important part of our having well-being in being human. It's that simple. And it's that important.'

Dan Siegel, author and psychiatrist

WHAT IS ATTACHMENT?

Attachment is about how it feels to be part of a relationship. This can be a couple relationship, a friendship, a relationship with a parent, or a relationship with your child. The quality of the attachment we experience is vitally important to our well-being. Relationships that feel bad can make us feel sick. One of the key researchers into the importance of attachment, particularly the attachment between parents and children, was Bowlby (1990). How relationships feel when you are in them links in a fundamental way to overall well-being. If a relationship with a person you spend a lot of time with is not giving you a good feeling then you will not feel so good overall. It is that simple and it is extremely important.

Think about the relationship you have with your child. When it comes to social media and being online, the quality of feeling they get from the relationship with you is one of the factors that will keep them safe or not. That's good news as most children have good quality attachments to their parents and feel good. But attachment is an issue that needs to be more fully understood as problems with attachment can cause problems online. The following needs to be understood:

- What impacts on attachment?
- How do attachments in our adult-to-adult relationships impact on how our children feel?
- Given that during adolescence children start to develop more emotional distance from their parents, generally speaking, how can you ensure that the attachment quality between you and your child is still secure?

We all live in relationships. Some are good for our health and some are not and how it feels to be in a relationship is what attachment is about.

What Is Secure and Insecure Attachment?

We all develop patterns of attaching in our adult-to-adult relationships and in our parent–child relationships. Attachments that are secure feel emotionally safe; you can say whatever you feel like saying to the person you are in the relationship with. Attachments that make you feel emotionally insecure and therefore leave you feeling like you need to be emotionally independent are insecure attachments. Only the people within any relationship can know how it really feels to be in it, and only you know how it feels to be in yours. That internal experience of a relationship is what attachment is. It is about what it feels like on the inside. Even when relationships end, strong attachments, just like strong feelings of love, can remain.

When it comes to your child's attachment to you, if they are open and honest and then start to become distant and less forthcoming it is worth checking in on the attachment, on how secure they feel about trusting you and leaning on you. You can do that by simply asking if they think they can trust you, if they think you are easy to talk to when they have issues they need to deal with. While adolescents tend to become more emotionally independent as they grow, you want them to still be able to fall back into your arms for emotional support if they need to. If the attachment relationship is good, that is more likely to happen.

When it comes to adult-to-adult relationships, it is important to be aware of the impact they have on children. If you feel insecure and unsupported in your couple relationship – because of troubles with intimacy or a lack of trust due to an affair for example – your child may notice the emotional distance their parents have from one another and believe that they need to be emotionally independent also. If you feel your own attachment with your partner is insecure you need to ask yourself if you could handle emotionally supporting your child if they need you too. If the answer is yes, then make sure your child knows that. Sometimes, children absorb beliefs from what they sense in their environment. If you have a secure attachment with someone else (for example, a sibling or friend), it could be that you have good emotional support although your child believes you have none. Tell your child explicitly that they can come to you and you will be able to handle anything they say. Stay tuned in too to what happens day-to-day in their online world. That way, you are showing with your actions that you are able to handle whatever is happening in their online world and they will build up trust in your ability to support them.

Adult-to-Adult Attachments

Aristotle once said that 'Knowing yourself is the beginning of all wisdom.' So for you as a parent it can be good and useful to look at your own main attachments. By taking a look at your own experience of relationships and how securely attached you are, you can become more self-aware and informed about what you bring to your relationship with your child.

When it comes to adult relationships, it is true that you can be in a relationship with someone without being really attached to them at all. You may feel as if you are in the relationship for practical reasons, rather than because the attachment or desire to stay there is strong. Also, you can be very attached to someone with whom you are not in a formal relationship. In that situation, your need for emotional support is being met but your children don't necessarily know that.

One of the indicators for working out who you're attached to in terms of your own adult relationships is to think about what you do during times of crisis; what person immediately comes to mind? Think back to a time when something went wrong. Who was the person you wanted to talk to there and then (even if you couldn't because you weren't in a relationship with them)? Who is it that you know that just by talking to that person you feel on steadier ground? Think about the people you are in relationships with: your spouse, sibling, friend. Are you likely to tell them straight away when things go wrong or do you tend to hold back for some reason? Attachment describes how it feels to be in a bond with another person, and secure attachment describes the feeling of safety you get within the relationship. For adults, the hope is that the person you are in an intimate relationship with is your secure attachment figure, but this is not automatically the case. If a child picks up on the fact that their parents do not lean on each other for emotional support they can be less likely to lean on their parents for support as they may believe (on an unconscious level) that their parents would not be able to cope with what they have to say. They may be right or wrong in that assumption, but it is not a great conclusion for a young person to come to. And because it is unconscious, the young person may not even be aware that that thought is there at all. So tell your child that you have support, and if you are a single parent, tell them too. Tell them you have emotional support and that you not being able to support them with stuff they are dealing with is not something they need to worry about. If it isn't from a spouse you get support, children may assume that you have none.

In order to be securely attached, you do not have to be in the same space as the person you are securely attached to, especially when you reach adulthood. But being in the same space for some amount of time is necessary to build attachment. And with parent–child relationships, being in the same space, most especially when children are small, really enhances attachment.

The Importance of the Child–Parent Attachment Bond

The attachment between a parent and a child right at the very beginning of the child's life matters most for well-being. This first experience of a relationship sets the scene for that child. It is their first and most formative experience of relationships. As babies we learn from those closest to us whether we can trust people to take care of us (or not). We also learn whether we can trust people to love us (or not). Babies learn this mostly from facial expressions, from how responsive their carer is to their needs in terms of going to them when they cry, from speaking to them in a soothing rather than a harsh tone. These very early experiences of what it feels like to be in a relationship with someone become the foundation upon which each person learns to attach. We (generally speaking) learn to trust or not trust. We (generally speaking) remain wary of others, or we are not wary. We either learn to fear closeness and intimacy, or we learn to embrace intimate bonds fearlessly. The attachments children experience in their earliest years can impact on their later attachments. So your early relationship experiences with your own parents matter when it comes to what you bring to the table when you in turn become a parent.

Because young people are beginning to use social media at an age when their main emotional relationship is still the one they have with their parents, you have huge potential influence. And because attachment is such a major part of keeping your child safe online, the best time to start thinking about attachment and how to make it secure is at birth. At the beginning of a child's life, a focus on attachment will be part of what prepares them for life online.

As young people grow and become adolescents, they are spending more time away from parents. But they can internalise the security from the attachment they have with their parents and as they go online, even if in a room by themselves, they are more likely to still feel emotionally safe because they know that their parent(s) have them in mind and are there for them. As teens are moving from childhood to adulthood but are not adults yet, they are still developing and therefore it is healthy for them if the secure attachment source (i.e. the parent) is physically around to some extent.

When it comes to mental health generally, good quality attachment matters. And when it comes to social media, young people are less likely to go off course, will be much more careful about who they are in contact with and will be more likely to recover well if something difficult happens if the quality of their attachment to their parents is good. If your child can lean on you for emotional support when times get tough, then they are more likely to form good quality bonds with others.

Young people are not tuned in to the type of attachments they have formed with their parents. They are focused on other aspects of their life and on other relationships as they grow up, particularly their relationships with peers. As the parent, you have to take the lead in order to give this some focus. By tuning in, you are working on a very important aspect of your relationship with your child which is protective of them.

Because all of us, as humans, are completely dependent on another for our very survival at birth, understanding attachment as a basic need for survival makes sense. From our earliest moments, all of us have an innate desire to attach. Our well-being depends on the quality of our connections with others.

Why Is Insecure Attachment Bad for You?

If young people have an attachment that is secure they are:

- More likely to manage conflict well
- Better able to manage difficult emotions that may arise
- Less likely to feel pressure to become sexually explicit in order to please others
- Less likely to keep secrets and feel they cannot share information with their parents
- More likely to treat people respectfully and honestly online
- Less likely to become dependent on feedback from others in order to feel good

Being in a relationship that doesn't feel good can erode self-esteem. This is especially true if you feel you are in a relationship with someone who is hostile towards you or doesn't really care if you're around or not. Ambivalence can leave you feeling unloved or rejected; hostility can leave you feeling under attack. And for adults who are in relationships where ambivalence or hostility features, you can sometimes find a way to normalise it; you may even source support outside of your main relationship. Imagine a child experiencing hostility or ambivalence, being shouted at or ignored. As a child, they may see this as a normal way to be treated in a close relationship and so that child could end up in a relationship as an adult where there is ambivalence or hostility too. It can become what a person expects, what they know and are comfortable with. Patterns develop; we all develop expectations, even if we're not consciously aware of them.

Relationships with poor attachments can cause stress, and can leave you feeling unappreciated or invalidated. And while some adults become used to that and just get on with things, for children it is damaging. It can feel like they are not able to fully be themselves within the relationship and it can compromise their ability to manage well online. Young people can feel as if they cannot fully express who they really are and so they are more likely to put on a show online in order to feel liked. Children pick up on the atmosphere in a home. Informing yourself as a parent about the attachments in the family is part of what will equip you with the ability to support your child to thrive. Good quality relationships matter for mental health and this is true whatever stage of life we find ourselves at.

ATTACHMENT QUALITY AND SOCIAL MEDIA

When it comes to social media, one of the main concerns parents can have is about secrets being kept or children doing things that might be considered dangerous. Attachment is directly relevant to that. Let's look at some of the specific apps and websites on which problems can emerge. As you look through the list of apps and the types of difficulties that can arise, know that good, secure attachment between you and your child will minimise any risk of danger.

- *Snapchat*: this is a messaging app in which the messages and photos disappear after a few seconds. The fact that the messages and photos disappear after a short space of time means that young people do not realise that sexts they send can be captured by screenshot. Young people tend not to think about the fact that their sexts can be stored and shared with others and this makes it potentially risky.
- *Kik*: this private messaging app allows people to send private messages that others cannot see. There is little that can be done to identify the person sending messages by Kik and so it is dangerous as your child can be in touch with people they do not realise pose risk. The fact that the messages can be sent secretly makes it attractive to some.
- *Whisper*: this social media site encourages people to post secrets. You can post anonymously but the location you are posting from is displayed, which can be very dangerous.
- *Fuckbook*: this site is used by adults to upload photos and connect in order to engage in sexual activity. It can be popular with some young people who are curious about sex and want to explore sex online yet it is extremely dangerous.
- *Yellow*: this app is meant to be for people aged 17 and over but it has become known as 'Tinder for Teens' and is proving popular

among young people in their early and mid-teens. It is often used to connect for casual sexual encounters.

These are only a few of the many apps and sites that parents may find it hard to monitor their child's activity on but, when it comes to explaining the dangers of these apps and sites to young people, if you and your child have a secure attachment then they are more likely to listen to and take on board what you have to say. They are also less likely to keep secrets from you (although it is normal for teens to want some level of privacy, they will not cut you out if you and they are securely attached). Because the internet and new apps are constantly being developed monitoring and filtering alone are never going to be enough to keep young people safe (although it is still necessary to monitor and filter). This is how good attachment helps.

If attachment between you and your child is secure, the outcome tends to be that:

- Your child is less likely to steer wildly off course and get into dangerous situations online (such as risky situations on apps/sites such as those outlined here).
- Your child is less likely to keep secrets about things that may be causing them distress (which is what every parent would want).
- Your child is more likely to feel confident and resilient when viewing the photos and content of others (which is immensely beneficial for self-esteem).
- Your child is more likely to feel confident when interacting with others online and uploading content (and therefore they are less likely to need validation so much).

When it comes to the teenage years, young people like to try things out and this involves taking some risks. Keeping some secrets is part of what is normal behaviour and this has always been the way. But there is a high level of risk potentially online and you can feel, because of sites such as those outlined here, at a loss as to how to keep your child safe. Secure attachment is one of the key ingredients for keeping your child safe. For example, research carried out by Rao and Madan (2013) in the Department of Psychology, Christ University, Bangalore, looked at the Facebook habits of young people and what difference secure attachment made to these habits. Even with this one social media app, there was a clear difference between the habits of those young people with secure and insecure attachments to parents. The insecurely attached adolescents 'showed patterns of low confidence and negative view[s] of others and situations' (p. 1). They did not like to be in contact with parents on Facebook and did not see it as a place for older people to be. This contrasted with the securely attached, who did not see privacy and independence as big issues, which would translate into them being ok with having their parents view their profile and be their 'friend' on Facebook. The securely attached adolescents 'enjoyed the presence of their family members on Facebook along with them' (p. 1). So secure attachment makes it more likely that your child won't mind your presence on social media, although they may have a strong opinion about you publicly commenting on their posts. Whatever the attachment style, a situation can still occur where a young person gets themselves into a dangerous situation online that they cannot see a way out of. They may feel embarrassed or afraid to come clean about what they have gotten involved in, but in this case, if the attachment with their parents is secure, they will be much more likely to feel that they can talk to their parents about the issue. This is especially true if you, as the parent, have already told your child that embarrassing or fear-provoking topics are ok to talk to them about. If the attachment within the relationship between you and your child is secure, the possibility of secrets being kept is greatly reduced. The level of risk to your child (of going off course, keeping things secret or feeling vulnerable and alone) is reduced and the level of open, honest communication increases.

Why the Quality of the Parent–Child Relationship Matters

Social media makes all sorts of relationships possible; and a lot of the connections can be with people the young person doesn't really know. Young people on social media want to feel good about themselves. They want to feel confident and strong, and with secure attachment to a main caregiver this confidence and strength is more likely. To begin to think about the current quality of the relationship with your son or daughter, imagine your child going on social media and asking themselves the following questions. Try to imagine the answers they would honestly give, as this will give an indication as to the current quality of the attachment between you.

- What if something happened to me online and I had to turn to someone?
- Could I talk to my parent/s?
- Do I really believe I could turn to them no matter what was going on?
- Do they usually listen when I have something I want to say?

The more positive the bond between a young person and their parents or carers, the more likely the young person is to handle well any difficult issues they face in the social media world, whether it be bullying, peer pressure, someone treating them badly, or them being at potential risk. Also, if your child is used to being in a relationship at home where communication happens well, where they can ask questions and negotiate their position without a row always being sparked, if they can talk without becoming aggressive or defensive, then they are more likely to communicate effectively and respectfully online.

Some parents find their teenagers are polite and respectful outside of the home and rude and disrespectful at home. While this is a difficult scenario to deal with, it can be resolved to a large extent by focusing on attachment. If a young person is hostile and aggressive at home – while it could indicate that they are not happy with the rules or not happy to comply with the limits you set – it can also be an obvious indication of emotional distress or unhappiness. Part of what could be going on is that the psychological task of identity formation is impacting on them in that they think their parents know nothing and don't deserve respect. (This can be a part of concrete thinking and moving away from what parents think in order to work out what they think themselves. The concrete thinking won't last forever.) So if this is what explains the behaviour, what can be done to prevent the attachment becoming insecure?

You could refer to the need for everyone in the house to be respectful of each other. Ideally, your tone of voice should remain calm as this is good for keeping attachment secure. You can comment on how your child seems to be annoyed, giving voice to their emotion in a soothing way. Focusing on your child's emotional experience rather than engaging in a battle with them will minimise any damage to their attachment. It is important to put boundaries and consequences in place around behaviours and state clearly what is acceptable and what is not when it comes to how your teenagers treat others at home. It is also important to validate their emotional experience, even if the emotion seems unreasonable. That way, you remain mindful and aware of attachment. Take the example of Jack, who has been pressing his girlfriend to send explicit pictures to him on Snapchat. His mother happens to see one of his messages as he was sending it and so she knows for sure he has done this. She tries telling him that it's not ok to pressure his girlfriend and he gets very angry and accuses his mother of interfering. This is the type of situation where attachment security can be threatened. It's tricky because his mother wants to give advice but also wants to make sure she doesn't damage her relationship with her son. She can say:

'I see you're upset and angry and that's hard for you. And I can understand that you feel that way because you think I'm trying to tell you what to do. Maybe I should have spoken to you a different way about it; maybe talking to you about your ideas about consent would have been better so that I can understand you. I don't want to interfere and I don't want you to feel you have to talk to me about everything but consent is a really important issue. Can we agree to disagree for now but talk about it another day this week? I want you to know you matter to me; otherwise I wouldn't be interested in having these difficult conversations with you. I want you to be happy. Do you know that? Do you believe me?'

If young people are used to the experience of being heard when they have something to say and if they are used to being encouraged to listen to another person's point of view, then they are much more likely to use these communication skills online. If you notice your child listening or communicating respectfully, you should praise them. It's good to emphasise how important these skills are. Tell them this is true online as well as at home and encourage them to keep that in mind. Hostility and a lack of compassion can make a person feel emotionally unsafe and if that is a feature of how you communicate it can undermine the quality of attachment between you and your child. Knowing this and discussing it with your child gives focus to the importance of keeping compassion centre stage. If communication is happening in a hostile way try hard to be the one who stays compassionate. Try not to join in with the hostility. It can be hard but knowing that hostility can undermine the emotional security your child feels can be your motivation to remain compassionate.

Visualising Social Media as a Fire-Prone Building

This simple visualisation is a way to understand what good quality attachment in the parent–child relationship can do when it comes to social media. Imagine social media is a building. It's a great place, a fun place with loads of opportunity to connect and have a positive impact on others. It's a building your child really wants to go into, but you know it could go up in flames. As their parent, you let them in there because it is how young people connect with each other in the world today. You want them to be connected and to have fun and you know that while there is a risk that the building will go on fire, it will probably be ok as they have protective armour on. So what do you do? Unless you go in there with them and watch every move they make (which most young people would not be happy with as they want independence as they grow and that's a reasonable expectation), you need another method of keeping them safe.

Step One: Preparation for Entering this Building Is Key

The best protective clothing to wear is confidence. The type of confidence that acts like protective clothing is internally sourced confidence. It has a reliable, internal source so it can be topped up if necessary by the young person themselves if it starts to spill out. The more of this they have, the better they will be able to keep safe and well on social media. See Chapter 2 for more on confidence.

Step Two: Know Where to Locate the Emergency Exit

The social media building is safe right now, but it could become dangerous if something goes wrong. If the building begins to burn, your child will need to get out of there fast to a safe place. Their protective clothing will not be enough to help them stay safe. They will need an emergency exit to get away from the danger. Therefore, they need to know where it is. So how do they figure out where the emergency exit is?

Upon entering the building, they need to be aware and look around. If they look to the window, they will see a strong, durable rope. This rope can be used to get out of that building to a place of safety. Your child can climb down the rope and can know always, when in that building, that the rope is there for them if they ever need it. Knowing this makes them feel more resilient and strong. It also helps you feel better about the fact that your child can get out of danger (and back to you) if things go wrong.

Note: If the young person doesn't know there is a safe place they can escape to, they will probably not even look for the rope or window and so their level of risk is higher.

Step Three: The Rope Analogy

It is extremely important to know that the rope is your child's attachment with you, their parent. The quality of that rope represents the quality of the attachment:

- Is it frayed and weak?
- Is it durable and strong?
- Can it keep them safe?

Your child needs to know this rope is there as they begin to use social media and you want to keep it durable and strong, even if the distance between you gets longer. No one can predict what might happen to a young person online; anyone can be bullied or feel tempted to go and do something risky. Your child needs to be aware that the rope is there for them to climb down. They need to know that they can get out of danger, get out of feeling unsafe and go back to a safe place (emotionally) if things start to get tough by talking to you about the problem or at least letting you know there is something wrong or they don't feel ok, even if that's all they are able to say.

Knowing the rope is there is that feeling your child can carry on the inside, a feeling of emotional safety, knowing their parent is there for them always. Children who have secure attachments are more likely to stay emotionally close to their parents, even during adolescence, and this closeness can really help if times get tough.

ATTACHMENT STYLES

What Is Meant by an Attachment Style?

An attachment style is thoughts, feelings and behaviours that become a pattern. People then display these thoughts, feelings and behaviours in close relationships and the other person's style interacts with it. If two adults with insecure attachment styles get together, neither one will seek support or be supportive of the other adult in the relationship. This may suit some people just fine as to be emotionally intimate can feel threatening. If one relationship a person is in is insecure, this does not mean that all of that person's relationships are insecure because the style of the person you are in the relationship with will influence your style. Just like with clothes, we all have a way of dressing that can be considered our style. Attachments are similar. And so they can change if we are influenced by the style of another or the style can remain constant.

Attachments are complex but there are basic principles that can be followed in order to increase the level of security. As young people starting to use social media are moving away emotionally from their parents and developing more emotional independence, secure attachment is optimal. Attachment can have an impact in a number of ways:

- *It impacts on how young people interpret things.* Attachment can influence how what is said by someone is interpreted and how the information that is taken into the brain through social contact with someone is processed and made sense of. For example, a young person who doesn't get a 'like' for a post from someone they really like could interpret that situation as either 'That must mean they like me; they're ignoring me as they want to play hard to get' or 'They mustn't like me at all.' Whichever way the interpretation happens is influenced by attachment. If a young person feels secure in their main relationship with their parents they will interpret things more positively or will bounce back more quickly than someone who thinks the opposite. This is because deep down their experience of their main relationship to date has taught them, at a very deep level, that they are likable and that belief exists at their very core.

- *It impacts on how they regulate and manage emotions.* Everyone has to deal with difficult emotions sometimes. How a person handles it – whether they can face into it head-on, or whether they try to escape from it/distract themselves from it – is influenced to some extent by their attachment and how secure they feel. The more secure a young person feels the better able they will be to face into and handle difficult emotions.

- *It impacts on how sexual development is perceived and how sexual relationships are approached.* If a young person has a secure attachment intimacy will not become something they grow up to fear and it will not become something they find difficult to manage. Also, if young people seek out sexual experiences rather than sexual relationships, a secure attachment with their parent will make it less likely that they will engage in behaviour that puts them at risk. That's good news when it comes to the area of sexting, meeting strangers or engaging in unsafe sexual sharing online.

For an attachment style to develop there needs to be a secure base. The stronger the secure base, the more secure the attachment becomes. A secure base is a place of emotional safety. It is an emotional space that is provided by one person to another (most usually in the context of a loving relationship) so that the person being provided with the space feels cared for, safe and loved. When you think of a toddler, that secure base may be physically in the arms of their parent and so when emotional safety is required, they go into the arms of their carer. As we grow, that emotional space can move to a place within ourselves. It then serves as a resource to us, even if the secure base provider is not physically around. A parent provides a secure base for their child, just as adults in intimate relationships can provide a secure base for each other.

Unlike how secure base provision can be in adult couple relationships (where each person provides a secure base for the other), secure base provision in parent–child relationships only works one way. Children don't (or at least should not as it's not healthy for a child) provide a secure base for their parent. The parents alone are the ones providing this emotional safe space, this unlimited emotional support. A secure base provides two things, which are connected:

- It is a secure base from which to go and explore the world and
- It is a safe haven which can be returned to when times get tough

This safe haven is one that becomes internalised over time. The internal sense of having a safe haven – knowing that your parent is there thinking of you, even if they are not physically around – can provide comfort for teens. Knowing that someone you love holds you in their mind and their heart, even if they are not there beside you, is central to having a secure base. After adolescence, the young person will likely go on to form other main attachments and therefore their secure base begins to be provided by someone other than the parent (perhaps a girlfriend/boyfriend or close friend).

If, as a parent, you have a secure base in someone else (for example, your spouse), it makes it more possible to provide a secure base for your child. If you do not have a secure base in your partner you can internalise a sense of a secure base from someone who has passed away to whom you were securely attached or you can have a secure base provided outside of your main relationship. If you don't have any secure base at all as a parent, your child can subconsciously pick up on that and this can cause them to rely less on you emotionally as they feel that you're unsupported.

It is important to allow your teenager a level of freedom to explore their world as this is how they figure out their place within it. Doing this safely is key and secure base provision will mean they are more likely to come back to base – back to you – particularly if things start to get difficult. That way, even if they meet new people or try new ways of being online they will remain connected with you. You will be more 'in the loop' or 'in the know' when it comes to what is going on in their social media world. They will be more forthcoming with you when it comes to questions such as:

- How did things go for you online today?
- Have you many friends on social media whom you have not met yet? What's that like for you?

This kind of conversation should be a normal part of family life. If your child shows some level of willingness to chat about these questions it indicates that a level of secure attachment is already present.

As already discussed, there are two main styles of relating to others, two main types of attachment styles, secure and insecure attachment. If your child has a secure attachment style in their relationship with you they will feel as if they can rely on you to be there for them, no matter what happens, and that will keep them psychologically safe to a large degree. If your child has a style of attachment that is insecure, that means they could either have a tendency to feel anxious (about being rejected or abandoned) or avoidant (of closeness and becoming dependent). There is no real way of knowing if your child not relying on you at all for emotional support is because of insecure attachment or because they feel ashamed or embarrassed about something unless you ask. Peer relationships take on great importance and can impact hugely on how and how much young people talk to parents. But it is worth having the conversation with them, perhaps acknowledging that they never rely on you for support and ask them why. Check how they feel about your relationship and use the rope analogy to explain how you want it to be. Even if they don't need you for support, there may come a time when they do. Make sure they understand that you want the rope – the attachment between you – to be durable and strong so that they can use it if they ever need to. Explain that you each hold the end of this imaginary rope. As your child grows they want to explore and so you give them more rope so that they can move further away from you. No matter how far away they go, the attachment keeps you connected. The state of the rope represents the state of the attachment and in order not to damage the rope you need to keep up communication. You also need to focus on making sure the communication is not hostile as this can be like a sharp knife fraying the rope.

Here are some general questions for your child to think about, if you want to talk to your child about their attachment with you:

- How would you describe the relationship you have with your parents right now: Close? Distant? Hostile? Warm?
- What do you think they would say about the way the relationship is?
- What do you think are the reasons for it being this way?
- Is it the way you would wish it to be?

Questions for you as the parent to consider:

- What do you know about your very early years? Was it a good time for you? How does it compare to the early years for your child?
- How would you describe the relationship you have with your teenage child right now: Close? Distant? Hostile? Warm?
- What do you think they would say about the way the relationship is?
- What do you think are the reasons for it being this way?
- Is it the way you would wish it to be?

By beginning to look at the relationship you currently have, you are beginning to focus on the nature of the attachment. It is like holding the imaginary rope between you and your child, looking at the state of the rope, examining how worn and frayed it is, how durable or not it is. It is a way of looking at how strongly or weakly you are connected, the connection being based on the condition of, rather than the presence of, the rope. And it is about identifying whether you want to stay where you are or improve the connection.

HOW ATTACHMENT MATTERS

Steve, age 14, is reluctant to talk to his parents about something difficult that is going on for him on social media. He is being bullied in school; people are messaging him to say 'Stay away from school. No one likes you anyway', and while he is confident and knows they are just being mean because of jealousy, it is starting to really get him down. John, his dad, knows Steve is holding back but cannot get him to open up, no matter how much he and his wife, Sophie, try to start a conversation about it. No matter how much they ask him if everything is ok, Steve just keeps saying, 'It's fine.' Here's one possibility as to what might be going on:

Unconsciously, Steve could very well believe that his parents would not be able to handle his problem. Possibly he is holding back because he has worked out unconsciously (which means he doesn't have awareness of this having been worked out in his mind, because it is below the surface) that his parents do not have a secure base in each other. He sees that his parents are not emotionally supported by each other. In then concluding that they don't have a secure base (maybe seeing that his mother does not lean on his father for support), he can believe (unconsciously) that neither parent is able to provide a secure base for him, even though they may wish to do so. What is sometimes not clear to young people is that adults have had a number of significant relationships in their life, with their co-parent, with siblings, friends, romantic partners, etc. Just because a parent may be in a relationship currently that does not feel secure in terms of secure base provision does not rule out the possibility that they have an internalised sense of security from a previous relationship experience or from a current relationship elsewhere. Therefore, it is important that Steve's parents are absolutely clear firstly with themselves about how their own attachment needs are met. Then they can say to Steve that he can always lean on them for support and they can handle anything. John or Sophie saying the following to Steve would help:

'You know you can talk to me about anything and I will be able to handle that ... do you think that's true?'

This is a way to bring unconscious beliefs up into the conscious mind so that they can be challenged. While Steve may not be talking because of other reasons, for example, he may think it will make things worse or he may be embarrassed, attachment is a potential major issue here and it is best to always stay mindful as to the influence of attachment.

Steve's mind is like an iceberg, as are all our minds. It is only the tip of the iceberg and the tip of the mind that is really known, unless you go down under the surface and start to explore your core beliefs. The part of the mind that is above water and can be seen is the conscious mind. The vast part of the mind that is beneath the water line is the unconscious part and while it may not be known, it has a massive influence on how a person feels and behaves. It is usually in that unconscious part of the mind that knowledge about attachment lies buried. It is only by bringing the information to the surface, like Steve's parents reassuring him that they can provide a secure base for him, that we have the power to change.

Young people whose parents seem to them to have insecure attachments and little or no support are usually less willing or able to use their parents as a secure base. This is not because they deem their parents to be uncaring. Rather it is because they absorb by osmosis the experience of being around that parent and have concluded (rightly or wrongly) that their parent would find it hard to act as a secure base for them. So if you find your child is not using you as a secure base, it could be that they have developed a belief in their unconscious mind (which could be incorrect) that you would not be able to cope with providing this emotionally secure, safe place. Maybe they feel you would be too overwhelmed with anxiety and therefore not able to support them with their emotional stuff. If that is the case, check with your child who they can talk to if things are hard for them. If it is not going to be a parent, make sure they have another adult they can trust and feel comfortable talking to, such as an aunt/uncle, family friend or professional.

If you can imagine being able to talk freely about attachment with your partner and how your needs are being met by each other, this would indicate that you feel there is a safe space (a secure base) there for you. If a conversation with your partner about attachment feels a bit risky, consider this question: Have you or your partner over time developed an attachment style together that is either anxious (the idea of closeness brings up a feeling of anxiety) or avoidant (emotional closeness is avoided)? Either situation can indicate insecure adult-to-adult attachment and so you need to focus that bit more on making sure your child knows that you can provide a secure base, an emotional place of safety, for them.

THE SECURE BASE

When it comes to any close relationships, there are two main features that are considered counterproductive to a solid secure base. Attachments between parents and children can be secure early in the child's life but as adolescence approaches and young people start to push boundaries they can become strained. That is why it is important to remain mindful of how important secure attachment is. A high level of hostility damages secure base provision so it is important to try to not become hostile, even if your child is really pushing your buttons. A low level of compassion also can undermine secure base provision so stay mindful of that too. If your child perceives you to be hostile or cold, they will be less likely to seek comfort or support from you. And this can be true even if you believe you are just being strict, not hostile. If your child, thinking in a concrete way, sees you as hostile, or if they get annoyed over not getting their way (for example, you put a limit on the amount of time they can be online in the evening), they can become the hostile one. It is important that as the parent you do not let this leave you feeling rejected or dismissed by your child. If you do, that also can undermine the secure base provision as you can withdraw a little bit emotionally in order to feel emotionally safe. Say something like:

'I know you are upset about only having half an hour to check your social media but I really feel that's the right amount of time for you, given everything else you have to do in the evenings too. I'm not going to speak to you in a hostile way and I'd appreciate it if you took the time to really think about the way you're speaking to me right now too. There will be many things we might disagree with as time goes on but I'd like if we could talk to each other without our relationship being damaged. You matter to me and I want you to know that. Even though you're angry right now, please be clear that this rule is not one that I am setting in order to annoy you. I am doing what I believe is best and after a few days, if it's really not working for you, come and tell me. We can look at it again and talk about it. I'll listen, I promise.'

This type of communication from a parent is optimal to protect the secure base. And as the provision of a secure base is one-way, the young person cannot be expected to take responsibility for fixing it. Hard as it can be, you, as the parent, need to take the lead and be the one to remain calm.

Hostility can sometimes be a mask for anger and anger can be a mask for fear or sadness. It is important that young people understand this and then think about what their own hostility, if they are being hostile, is really about. After an explosion of hostility from your teenager, once things have calmed down, you can suggest that you and your child think together about what underlying feeling they may have been having when they became hostile and why. Similarly, if you, the parent, have become hostile, that can be examined too. Even if young people are not willing to discuss hostility it is good for them to reflect and be encouraged to think about it a bit. This talking about it creates a space for compassion to come back in. And this is a clear route out of a hostile communication pattern. The above is an example of how a young person's hostility can be a mask for fear and sadness. Maybe she thinks that if she isn't online for the same amount of time as her friends in the evening she will begin to be left out or forgotten about by her peer group. If you communicate in a way that makes space for your child to feel calm, perhaps at a later time of the day or on the next day they can talk about what could have been underneath the hostility; this can be really helpful for your child. In this example, you can ask your child, 'Why were you so angry about having to go off Snapchat last night?' and your child can say, 'I feel like I'll miss something if others are on there and I'm not and I worry they won't miss me', then the opportunity to talk about this worry and perhaps a feeling of insecurity can be addressed. Young people can become addicted to their social media devices quite quickly. It is good for them to be aware that this can happen and again, if attachment is secure, your child will be more willing to listen when you talk about why it's important to take breaks from being online. (For example, it gives them a chance to interact with family members, to engage in something they love doing, to pursue a hobby or to enjoy their own company for a while). Having the space to talk will give them the chance to work out this underlying insecurity about their position in relation to their friendship group.

Boundaries are useful even if your child is hostile in how they communicate about the boundaries you set. It is normal for young people to try to push against boundaries but disagreeing does not have to inevitably lead to hostility and lack of compassion, once you keep in mind the need to stay calm and lead by example. If young people are becoming hostile, this needs to be dealt with. You can express a clear expectation that hostility is not acceptable. You can say:

'I make an effort to talk to you in a way that is respectful and not aggressive and I expect you to do the same. It's fine if you're angry but you do not need to be aggressive. You need to try to speak to me in a way that is not aggressive and then I will really listen to what you want to say.'

Eye contact while communicating this type of message can also help. And while it can be intense for young people to look someone in the eye while something hard is being said, it can really strengthen the link with them during the interaction. With younger children, eye contact is something they generally engage in and enjoy when it is encouraged by parents. For older children, particularly when they gain access to screens, eye contact can greatly diminish. Eye contact with someone you care about releases oxytocin, a natural anti-anxiety and anti-depressant hormone, and it has the effect of lifting a person's mood. Oxytocin also has the capacity to intensify the bond you feel with someone and it can promote secure attachment. Even if you are not discussing anything with your child, perhaps if they come in for dinner and sit down try to encourage or even request some eye contact. While it may feel unnatural or weird if it is not something you are both used to doing, it is a very simple and effective strategy that works well to build up the bond. For young people who are spending a lot of time looking at screens, it is important that there are times when screens are put away and space is made for eye contact. Perhaps introduce a rule to say no screens at the table during mealtime or no screens when you sit down to chat. Eye contact between you and your child should become part of their daily diet. That way, the secure base can be strengthened but they also get the opportunity to naturally produce oxytocin in their body.

ATTACHMENT AND EXCLUSION ONLINE

What Should I Do if My Child Is Excluded Online?

You cannot control how other people treat your child online and, yes, they could experience being excluded or feeling excluded. They may not be invited to a party, which can be hard enough, but then they see photos from the party posted on Snapchat which can compound the feeling of being left out. They could post a selfie or a status update on Facebook which is then largely ignored by some friends; they can be left out of a group chat and not know why. Exclusion, if faced by young people on social media, could result in their unconscious mind dealing with two competing unconscious thoughts:

- I need to protect myself from the pain of this and therefore disconnect from others and/or
- I need to connect with someone who will make me feel emotionally safe

It is important to listen to your child explain how they feel about their experience of exclusion, rather than just focus on the facts of what happened. They may feel fine about it and recover really quickly or they may feel rejected and their confidence can drop. You need to stay tuned in to how the experience is making them feel about themselves, which is a step towards helping them maintain their confidence. It is important that focus is given to confidence so that it can be protected. By supporting them to see that it is the person doing the excluding (if they have done it in an intentional, mean way) who has the issue, you are giving your child a valuable perspective that can help them maintain their confidence. It can be hard to deal with feeling excluded, especially if it happens a lot. Help your child become aware of their own actions online too in order to ensure they are not causing pain intentionally or unintentionally by excluding others. You can do this by asking about what they are posting and then asking them to imagine what the person receiving that text/comment/response may feel. When someone is left out of a conversation on Snapchat or if a post they have shared about themselves on Facebook is deliberately ignored or ridiculed it can be difficult to handle.

If attachments are not secure and there is no internalised sense of security, a young person can often find it more difficult to cope if something painful is going on. Young people can use unsafe ways to try to cope with distress, such as turning to alcohol, drugs or self-harm. They can take unsafe actions impulsively during times of distress, before even thinking it through. But attachment can and does play a part. You can say to your child:

'If you ever feel like you are in a situation that is really hard and you don't know what to do or how to cope, I want you to be able to come to me. Don't ever feel as if you need to do anything like harm yourself or turn to alcohol or drugs as a way to try to manage difficult emotions. Those methods don't ever work and only cause more pain. Please know that no matter how bad things get or how bad you may feel, I'll be there. Hopefully you will never feel bad but sometimes people do so I'm saying it just in case.'

There is something good about saying this explicitly and a good chance to say it can arise if you are aware your child is dealing with something that upsets them in even a minor way online. Adolescents with avoidant attachment styles (who avoid closeness in order to avoid the risk of being let down) tend to try to remain independent emotionally. And while emotional independence is something that all young people growing up will be developing, keeping a complete emotional distance from everyone – a distance which is fuelled by a rigid need to be independent and self-sufficient – can be a risk to one's well-being. By not seeking support from anyone, feelings of distress can become overwhelming.

As young people go through adolescence and towards adulthood, their main attachments will gradually transfer onto other people their own age and away from you as their parent. This is a normal part of growing up and can be talked about with your child. Be clear in your own head though that this move towards independence does not mean that the attachment between you and your adolescent has to become insecure. Take the lead in minding the security of their attachment relationship with you. There is the opportunity for you to continue to provide a secure base to your adolescent child as they grow and this will not only help keep them safe online, but it will have a positive effect on their developing close relationships with others into the future too.

Section II

MANAGING WHEN TIMES GET TOUGH

4

STEP FOUR: KNOWING HOW TO MANAGE DIFFICULT EMOTIONS

'Feelings are something you have, not something you are.'

Sharon L. Alder, author

WHAT ARE DIFFICULT EMOTIONS?

There are many different kinds of emotions but difficult ones, in the main, are those that are not necessarily welcomed or enjoyed by the person feeling them. They are what some people might refer to as 'negative' feelings, and while no feeling is fully positive or negative, they all just 'are', some feelings can seem negative because they are difficult to bear and express. Anger, frustration, anxiety, sadness, hopelessness, jealousy, resentment – while these are all within the range of what is normal to feel, they can be difficult to experience. And if these emotions become really big for a young person they can overwhelm them. When feelings become unbearable or overwhelming, and are combined with a young person's tendency to be impulsive, certain scenarios become very risky. Also, if a young person is on a mobile device and, for example, gets a nasty comment, they are often on their own at the time. That is why it is essential for young people going online to have coping skills that will support them to manage such 'difficult' emotions.

CONSIDERING IMPULSIVITY

While impulsivity is not an emotion, it is an important topic to discuss with your child before they go online. Impulsivity and the tendency for some young people to become more impulsive during adolescence create a context for managing difficult emotions that needs to be understood. A tendency towards impulsivity is a tendency to act without thinking, to just go ahead and do something, say something or post something online without really thinking it through first. This impulsivity can be a feature of adolescence because of the particular stage of development adolescents are at. They can tend to act without thinking to a much greater extent than adults.

This impulsivity can cause difficulty not just for the young person themselves but for others too, perhaps the person on the receiving end of their comment or the person whose compromising picture they just shared. Therefore, impulsivity is absolutely something that young people need space to talk about. Part of them being able to manage their social media use involves being aware of the danger of acting impulsively when they are feeling overwhelmed with anger, sadness or anxiety, for example. This awareness will help keep them safe online. If they lack awareness, they or others can get hurt if they say or do something impulsively that causes harm in some way.

If young people don't learn how to manage difficult emotions, they can become unbearable or the feeling, unexpressed, can get stuck. This can be a contributing factor for all sorts of difficulties, such as:

- Depression
- Anxiety
- Eating disorders
- Lack of concentration
- Withdrawing from friends
- Social difficulties
- Self-loathing
- Self-harming
- Alcohol or drug use as a way to escape
- Over-sexualised behaviour
- School refusal
- Hostility in family relationships

Young people are more likely to engage in dangerous or unhealthy behaviours as a way of trying to escape the difficult feeling if they don't feel able to manage it. And it can be hard for parents to really know how their child is coping emotionally unless they are specifically asking about feelings on a regular basis. Often mental health problems are difficult for parents to spot straight away, especially if the young person is reluctant to talk. It is necessary to equip your children with at least some level of skill to manage emotion.

It is not immediately obvious when you look at someone what state their mental health is in and it is common for mental health difficulties to remain hidden for a time. A mental health issue is different from a broken leg or a fractured arm. You can immediately see from someone's outward appearance whether they are dealing with a physical injury or not. But you can't see into someone's mind. Just as anyone can break a leg, anyone too can have mental ill health. And because of that fact, it is important that young people online know how to mind their mental health.

All sorts of things impact on mental health. Experiences influence how a person feels but how a person feels is much more influenced by their *interpretation* of that experience. How a young person thinks about themselves, how their experiences influence them to think about themselves, how their beliefs about themselves and the world are developing – these aspects can all impact on their mental health. So being able to care for their mental health is about learning how to stay strong in their mind. Being tuned in to their own confidence source and thinking in a way that is encouraging and supportive of themselves is something that will set the young person on a path to positive mental health. While difficult situations arise for young people on social media sites, the young person who has prepared and has skills to handle these difficult experiences and feelings will be more resilient in facing the difficulties. There is a lot young people can learn about minding their mental health. And knowing these skills, having the tools, places them in a much stronger position online.

In all aspects of life, difficult feelings can arise. This is true at every age, for children, adolescents and adults alike. It can be hard at any age to feel anger, hurt, sadness or worry but having a strategy to deal with difficult feelings is one thing that puts a person in a better position. This doesn't mean the person won't feel the hurt, sadness, worry, etc., but it means it is less likely to overwhelm them and cause them to use dangerous coping mechanisms. Difficult feelings can arise quite suddenly online and it can be hard for young people to know what to do.

DIFFICULT FEELINGS AND SOCIAL MEDIA

When young people go onto social media sites they enter a very public space and yet they are usually still quite alone. That makes them vulnerable. There are all sorts of situations and feelings that can arise at any point online. Feedback is immediate and fast and not always positive. Young people also have access to all sorts of information and images of others which may intensify a negative feeling they already have about themselves. They may feel compelled to go onto certain sites in order to work out what others think of them; for example, a young person who is socially active and engaged with friends can feel the need to join Instagram because all her friends are on it and, once on there, there is pressure to get followers and be 'liked'. Young people need to be equipped with knowledge about how to mind their feelings online. They need to know the importance of paying attention to how they are feeling and they need to have a strategy if the feeling becomes very difficult to manage. This will increase their resilience and will in turn help keep them safe from harm.

Posting Mean Comments

As a parent, you have an important role to play in helping your child treat others well online. As some young people are accessing social media sites before they even reach adolescence you need to recognise that this means your child is limited in terms of how much they can think in an abstract way, which means they are limited in their ability to see things from another person's point of view. Take, for example, a ten-year-old boy who thinks it's funny to post an image of his friend doing something stupid that he himself finds funny. It would not be unusual for this ten-year-old to have no awareness whatsoever of the fact that his friend may be embarrassed or humiliated to have this photo shared. The boy sharing the image is not a 'mean' child; he just is at a stage of development that limits his ability to empathise with how others feel, especially in the moment of doing something that excites him. You can educate your child about the need to show respect and kindness towards others online by, for example, explaining to them how posting that 'funny' image could upset the other child. Children need to be told that others, as well as themselves, can tend to be impulsive and act quickly. This can give them a context for understanding how a friend who seems to have done something mean is not necessarily intending to be mean at all. It can also help them to think before acting too quickly and posting a comment without thinking. Talking about impulsivity gives your child the chance to think not just about the potential consequences for themselves (for example, they get labelled a bully) but also about the possible consequences for the other person's feelings. It is only through bringing this into the conversation at the very beginning of a young person's engagement with social media that their awareness will start to develop. Talking about simple, everyday situations, such as the one outlined above, with your child will help increase their awareness. But it needs to be brought into the conversation on a regular basis in order to have real impact. Young people sometimes spend a lot of time online so it takes time and effort to ensure that your child's habit of engaging respectfully online is fully formed.

An Action Plan for Managing Difficult Situations

Creating a plan of action for managing difficult emotions is a very practical and useful thing to do. This plan is something that can be known to your child and used by them when times on social media become tough. It can be described best as a plan that they can follow if they have a feeling that is hard for them to deal with. You can explain that difficult feelings are a part of life but on social media, because their focus is on the content of what they are absorbing or viewing online (something outside of themselves), their focus is often not on how they feel (which is about their inner life). This is why it is so important to talk about this issue ahead of time, preferably before your child starts to use social media at all. Once your child is socialising online, they become distracted by the content of what they are seeing and saying. Their focus is on something 'outside the self' while what they feel when online is very much 'inside'.

When discussing making this action plan, you can talk about some of the feelings that may prompt its use, such as sadness, worry, hurt, anxiety, anger, fear or embarrassment. Your child may not associate these feelings with social media but you can say that while social media can be fun it can at times be hard and it is necessary to be prepared for such situations. Ask your child if they know anyone who ever had a hard time on social media and they may well be able to come up with some examples themselves. It is important to talk to your child about this as young people tend not to think ahead to times that may be difficult online. And while you don't want to ruin your child's excitement about accessing the social media world, it is necessary that they are properly prepared. By having this conversation their awareness about the need to tune in to how they are feeling is increased. When young people pay more attention to how they are feeling their level of resilience will increase. Even a simple example of getting really mean comments on a picture posted could be an example to get started. Ask your child how they think someone should cope with that. Perhaps they should pause and check in with how they are feeling inside. Explain how this is the first step in minding their confidence and managing any sadness. A simple conversation like this can make the issue more real.

The action plan of how to manage difficult feelings should contain steps your child can take when they begin to notice that they do not feel ok. They need to know:

- How to pause and work out what they are feeling
- What is causing the feeling
- What they can do about it

Implementing the Action Plan – Some Case Studies

If your child is not taught to pause and tune into what they are feeling, they will not be likely to do it, especially once they go online. You can use the case study below to show your child how this process works. Using case studies like these makes the concepts easier to grasp. Once you read the example, ask your child to try to tune into how Sam might be feeling.

SAM AND THE PARTY

Sam's friend was having a party. Sam knew that he probably wouldn't be invited as he made friends with and was invited to the house of the new boy in their class last week. His friends didn't seem pleased about this and Sam has a feeling he would not be invited to the party as a result.

While Sam knew deep down his friend would probably exclude him, it didn't make it any easier when it came to the time of the party. And seeing the photos on Instagram of his friends having fun made it even harder. 'Why could we just not all be friends: them, me and the new boy?' Sam thought. 'Why are they being so mean to me when I haven't done anything mean to them ever?' Sam had only wanted to make the new boy feel welcome and now it felt as if he was being punished.

With this example, your child needs to learn the following:

- Sam is probably feeling a mixture of emotions (anger, sadness, hurt, etc.) and this is normal.
- Naming the different feelings is part of what helps Sam feel better. Naming the feelings is a step towards managing them. It is a part of what young people need to do when things get tough.

Once the feelings are known, the next step is to work out what is causing the feeling and what can be done about it. A large part of what causes us to feel certain things is our perception of events and so by giving focus to perception a young person can get control over what way they are interpreting events and how they can think in a different way (i.e. change their perception) in order to feel differently. So Step Two (working out what is causing the feeling) and Step Three (working out what can be done about it) involves a focus on perception. Perception is the way a person interprets or sees something. There are two possibilities for Sam when it comes to perception:

- Sam sees the others all having fun and feels very sad and upset. He thinks they don't like him anymore and he loses a lot of confidence. He starts to wonder if anyone will like him ever again or if he will end up with no friends at all.

- Sam feels annoyed and hurt and sees how unfairly his friends are treating him. But he thinks they will all be friends again, once he talks to them about it and explains how it made him feel. He will talk to them about it and try to work it out with them, maybe listening to how they felt when he became friendly with the new boy. Maybe they were hurt then or jealous. He is not going to worry because he knows these things happen to almost everyone. It's a normal part of growing up.

The important point for your child to know and understand from this is that how a person feels when something happens is influenced hugely by their perception of what has happened rather than by the event itself. It is crucial that children understand what perception means. Here's an example to illustrate the importance of perception.

LILY AND TOM

Sixteen-year-old Lily is dumped by her boyfriend, Tom. All her friends know before she does because Tom changed his Facebook status to 'Single' before letting her know he was ending the relationship and she hasn't really been on Facebook. Others see this before Lily does and tell her on Snapchat.

Perception One

Lily feels mortified, hurt, humiliated. She cannot believe that Tom would treat her this way and cannot stop thinking about what everyone must think of her now. She wants to hide away, not go to school, not face people. She begins to feel really bad inside and begins to wonder if she is perhaps worthless. How could she be anything other than worthless if someone treats her so bad? Lily feels the embarrassment is becoming too hard to bear. She doesn't know how to stop the feeling and she wants it to stop.

Perception Two

Lily sees this as disrespectful behaviour. While she can see that Tom is entitled to end the relationship if he wishes to, he did it in a public way that could have left her feeling exposed, vulnerable and humiliated, and, according to Lily, this makes Tom undesirable, disrespectful and immature. He could have ended the relationship differently but, as Lily perceives it, Tom has shown his true colours. He was nasty and while Lily is feeling hurt by the event and angry at Tom, she also feels glad that she is no longer Tom's girlfriend as she now sees him as an idiot.

The clear message is that perception shapes how people feel. Perception will shape your child's reality.

Awareness of the Power of Perception

Young people (and some adults too) are generally not aware of the power of perception and how much it shapes how they see things and how they feel. Beck (20011) has written extensively about the link between what we feel and what we think. His theory has developed into a therapy known widely as cognitive behavioural therapy. Your child needs to learn about the power of perception in order to be in charge of minding their mental health online.

Young people going online need to think about their mind as if it was a muscle. If they think of it in that way they will feel more powerful in relation to making their mind strong. By taking time to pause and think about how they feel about and how they perceive something, your child can build up strength in this muscle and they can then develop a stronger, more resilient mind. This will be extremely helpful when difficult feelings arise. And for everyone there comes a point when a difficult feeling arises.

Perception is influenced by a person's thoughts. And confidence is something that impacts a lot on how a person thinks. Because a lot of thoughts happen automatically, especially for a young person on social media, it is important that your child learns to pause. Their inner source of confidence comes into play here as the more your child is confident because of confidence sourced from the inside the more likely they are to perceive events in a way that works well for them. So Lily, believing she is better off without someone who can treat her as badly as Tom did, is demonstrating good internal confidence. She is demonstrating that she knows she deserves better than to be treated that way.

THE LINK BETWEEN FEELING AND THOUGHT

Once your child knows:

- What are the things that make them feel better
- How to tune into what they are feeling
- How to work out what way they are interpreting things (i.e. their perception)

they are ready to move on to the next step. This next step is understanding the link between a feeling and a thought. If your child understands this link and is able to pause, it will help them to work out why they feel as they do. This is necessary in order to manage the difficult feeling.

We all, as adults, give meaning to events that happen in our lives and we do this on a daily basis. We do this so automatically sometimes (i.e. unconsciously) that it is often the case that we don't realise that the meaning we prescribe to an event is based on our perception of events and our interpretation. So two people going through exactly the same event can have totally different emotional reactions to that exact same event; this is demonstrated in the two hugely different outcomes in how Lily could feel about being dumped by Tom in the example above.

It can be particularly hard during adolescence to get to grips with the idea of different perceptions as a lot of thinking is still happening in a concrete way. So your child may see things as black and white. They may not see that there is another way to look at things. Take the example of Sam again, feeling annoyed and hurt by being left out by his friends. With Perception One, thinking he may never have friends again, this thought will probably lead to hopelessness. With Perception Two, where he feels things will probably work out ok, this thought will lead him to feel hope. It's the exact same scenario but different thoughts lead to very different feelings.

Understanding the Importance of the Link between Thoughts and Feelings

It is vital that you, as the parent, explain the important link between how a person feels and how a person thinks to your child. Once the link between thought and feeling is understood, your child has this powerful knowledge: they can influence then how they feel by making a choice about what they are thinking. It is clear that by changing what you think you can change how you feel, but this is often easier said than done. That is because the thoughts become set in patterns over time and ways of thinking become a habit. So what is it that influences these patterns of thinking that we all fall into? It is our beliefs that influence the way we tend to think (whether we are usually optimistic, fatalistic, self-critical, etc.). And for your child online, be well aware that their beliefs are still forming.

Beliefs and Their Power

Beliefs are not facts. You may believe you're no good at something but really the belief is subjective and someone else may have a different view. If your child believes something long enough it can feel like a fact to them. And unless conversations happen about their beliefs, they can go online without any sense of what they believe about themselves, the world and the people they know in it. As beliefs are at the root of thoughts and thoughts influence how a person feels, your child will greatly benefit from looking at some of the core beliefs they are developing as they are about to go online. This will help them manage their feelings if times get tough.

Beliefs about Yourself

Going back to Sam and Lily, both of those young people could either believe good things about themselves or not. In one scenario, Sam could believe that he is a good friend, worth having as a friend and that he is a kind person. This belief will influence him to think in a hopeful way about working things out with his friends. If he is not so positive about himself, if he believes that maybe he is not that likeable, maybe he is not worth having as a friend, he will be more likely to think that his friends wouldn't want him around anymore. So what Sam believes about himself is at the core of how he ends up feeling.

For Lily, she could have a belief that she deserves to be treated with respect. This will influence her to think that Tom was way out of line in how he acted towards her. If she does not hold this belief though, she will be more likely to feel humiliated and self-loathing, beginning to develop a new belief perhaps that no one can be trusted or that she needs to change herself in order to impress others.

It is important to check on a fairly regular basis what your child believes about themselves. Their beliefs are only developing and incidents that happen with peers can influence your child's developing beliefs about themselves without them even knowing. It is optimal for mental health if your child can look inward themselves at their developing beliefs. They can ask themselves questions such as:

- What did seeing that/hearing that/having that event happen make me think about myself?
- What does it make me believe about myself?

You can help by asking:

- What did that event/that person saying that make you think of yourself?
- What do you think makes you a good person/a good friend?

If your child doesn't learn the value of doing this self-reflecting they can begin to feel bad if they interpret or perceive things in certain ways. This can happen even if they are not interacting with others socially as they can be scrolling through content and comparing themselves (unconsciously) to others online. If they are not paying attention to how this is making them feel about themselves, they are running the risk of eroding their self-esteem or believing they need to present themselves in a particular way in order to be deemed 'of worth' and they can become a bit narcissistic.

IMPULSIVITY AND SOCIAL MEDIA

With social media, scenarios arise which lead to young people making decisions quickly without the support of a parent. This is normal for young people and a necessary step for them to take towards independence; they have to be able to learn to manage things themselves. And part of that move towards independence means making a decision alone. So let's assume that your child will find themselves in a situation where they need to make a decision that could, if they don't learn how to pause, be an impulsive one. A decision regarding sexual conduct is an example of when behaviour can become impulsive. When sexually aroused, it is harder for people to think clearly and pause. This makes it more likely that impulsivity comes into play.

Managing their sexual self (how they present themselves sexually and how they engage with others sexually) is a part of social media life that young people need to know about and be somewhat prepared for. For adolescents, even when they know the consequences of doing something could be serious they may go ahead and do it just because of their tendency to seek a thrill in the moment. This adrenalin rush that your child can get when they do something thrilling or risky can be felt very intensely. It can be a part of the context for their apparent lack of caution. If the experience that is available to them to engage with is something novel then the intensity of feeling can be even stronger. It can seem 'out of character' for some but any young person is capable of impulsive action, and if a young person is with their peers the intensity of the feel-good factor can be felt even more. This is true even in situations where the young person is aware that the potential consequences may be serious. It is a normal part of growing up to act impulsively but there are ways to prepare young people to deal with situations which should help to keep them safe.

Step One: Knowledge Is Power

You can explain to your child, as they are approaching adolescence, that when people their age do something new and novel, even if it is something they know is potentially risky, their brain releases a chemical, oxytocin, that makes them feel good. This is part of being a teen and it is related to biology rather than who they are as a person. And if this novel or risky act is being performed in front of peers, there can be an even more intense feel-good factor with more oxytocin being released. When adolescents know this it does not act to excuse impulsive behaviour. Rather, you can state an expectation that your child pause and tune in to this feeling that is being released inside. Paying attention to it and being aware of it gives them the option to take more control of it.

Step Two: State an Expectation that They Will Pause and Think

You can tell your child that while they will get to make their own decisions, and to make their own mistakes, you expect them to at least pause and make the decision through thinking, tuning in to what they feel and what they think, rather than just acting on impulse all of the time. Impulsivity in and of itself may not be considered to be a risk but acting impulsively can lead to situations that further down the line cause your child and others distress. Talk to your child about their digital footprint and how every action they take online is part of the footprint they leave there forever, for others to potentially see. Your child needs to know about impulsivity and how to manage it ahead of time.

IMPULSIVITY, SEXTING AND SELF-WORTH: CASE STUDIES

Below are some examples of situations online where young people can either act impulsively or they can decide to pause to think. These are examples you can use with your young teen as a way to talk about impulsivity as they are quite typical of scenarios that can arise on social media. And while your child cannot be told how to act, pausing to work out what they feel and what they think makes them more likely to choose behaviours that are safe for them.

ADAM AND THE EXPLICIT IMAGE

Adam is a fourteen-year-old boy in school. He is on social media during his lunch break and sees that his friend has shared a naked picture of his girlfriend, Sue. A lot of the boys, including Adam, fancy Sue. Adam knows this is a very mean thing his friend has done but he really fancies Sue and would love to save the image. He reckons no one would have to know. He is worried though. Adam knows (because his parents told him) that to have sexual images of other people his age means his phone potentially has child pornography on it. He doesn't know what to do, and doesn't want to be in trouble.

This situation is a challenge for Adam. He needs to figure out what to do. He works out a plan about what to do about this difficult feeling of 'confusion'; his plan is to pause and focus on his thoughts and feelings.

Adam's Feelings

* Worry

Thoughts: If I save the photo and my parents find out I could be in a lot of trouble. I don't know what my parents would think about me looking at a picture like that or saving it. Sue didn't even mean for me to see it. She did not give consent for anyone else to see it and so I know I absolutely don't have Sue's consent to view or save the image. I'm worried that saving the image would upset and anger her. And even if she was my girlfriend, my parents have warned me about naked pictures. I am worried too because if my friends find out I haven't saved it, they may think I am not at all cool.

* Confusion

Thought: This is tough; I really don't know what to do.

* Excitement

Thought: I have access to explicit sexual content of this girl I really like.

Adam looks at his specific thoughts.

Adam's Thoughts

* I would love to see the photo.
* I know consent really matters.
* I don't want to get into trouble with my parents.

- I don't want child pornography on my phone.
- I don't want to risk being seen as a loser by my friends.
- I am really confused.
- I don't want to be disrespectful to Sue.

By identifying his thoughts, Adam then has the chance to make up his mind about what matters the most. Does he believe that if he does something his friends think is uncool then they will dump him as a friend? Or could he explain himself by saying that having a naked picture of a fourteen-year-old girl could get him into trouble with the authorities? Adam has to work this out for himself, just as each young person has to work out their own decisions. But emphasising the importance of respect for other people and other people's online data is extremely important. If conversations are not happening about the need to not share other people's data without their permission or consent, then young people are not getting the chance to learn about the issue of consent. That is extremely dangerous.

By going through this type of example with your child, you are giving them the following messages:

- As your parent, I know this type of situation arises.
- I am fine with talking about issues about sexual conduct.
- I am knowledgeable about the law and want you to be too.
- Being respectful of other people is absolutely paramount.
- Consent matters when it comes to the sharing of images.
- I expect you to pause and think. I expect you not to act on impulse as it is not safe.

In this situation, or any situation similar to it, your child will have to make their own mind up about what to do. You cannot dictate to them, although you can put time and effort into helping your child prepare for these situations by, for example, talking about consent. Through you asking your child what they think Adam should do, you are giving them a good opportunity to prepare well to deal with situations that might cause them confusion. In this situation, Sue has not given consent for Adam to view or store the image of her. It is vital that Adam understands that consent is a key issue in this decision-making process as Sue deserves his respect.

Giving Some Focus to Consequences

While everyone is different, most young people will understand Adam's feelings and thoughts. Whatever way they might act in a situation such as this, it is important for your child to have the opportunity ahead of time to look at the potential consequences of their actions. This can be done by looking at the potential consequences for Adam.

Explain to your child that how Adam feels is because of what he is thinking. While he wants to see that photo as he really likes Sue, it's good that he is taking the time to think it through first and not just acting on impulse. Emphasise that Adam is being careful about his actions and this is important as there can be serious consequences if you act impulsively and view particular sexual content online. Reiterate again the danger of:

- Sending sexual images (you cannot control where these images may end up and they could end up being used by someone whom you don't want using them)
- Receiving sexual images (there is a risk of it being considered child pornography if the image is of a young person)
- Disregarding consent (consent was not given for the image to be shared and therefore it should not be shared)

Viewing sexual images of adolescents could, depending on the age of the person in the photograph or video, and the age of the person in receipt of it, be construed as child pornography. Therefore, a young person who is passing around an explicit sext they received could be distributing child pornography, depending on the age of the young person in the image. Young people are generally not aware of this and are not aware of the serious consequences of being found to be in possession of, or distributing, child pornography. Discussing this example is an opportunity to educate your child about this important fact.

The purpose of working through this example is for your child to have practice at pausing and working out what they are thinking. Your child doesn't have to solve Adam's dilemma for him but it might be good to ask your child if they think they would find this type of situation hard. Working through the above stages will help them see the link between how a person feels and how they think. This will remind them to hit pause on their actions when they face their own dilemmas online. They can simply say to themselves:

- I need to pause.
- What am I feeling?
- What am I thinking?

As a parent, you know that sexting is a part of teenage culture and even before the age of thirteen young people can sometimes feel pressure to sext. Because it is something that you as a parent did not have to deal with when you were a teenager it can be hard to know how to introduce the topic with children. You can introduce the topic of sexting by talking firstly, in a more general way, about situations that can lead to difficult feelings arising on social media, perhaps in a group chat: someone says something mean to someone else and you don't know whether to defend them, pretend you don't see it or go offline altogether for a while. After this more general example about how things can be a bit tricky, you can bring up the specific example of a situation where a young person feels pressure to send a sexual image of themselves, for example, a selfie of them in their underwear, and that because it can be hard to know what to do you want to talk to them about ways to deal with that.

Setting a time aside to go through an example of what can happen is a good idea. The fact that the case study is about someone else and not your child should help them explore their ideas without it feeling too personal to them. The story of Emily and the sexts below is one that can be used to explore this issue. Read through the next case study together and ask your child to try to identify and name the feelings Emily might have, in the same way they did for Adam above. If your child is reluctant, you can offer some suggestions. (It's good to work out this example with both boys and girls as the issue affects both genders).

EMILY AND THE SEXTS

Emily is thirteen years old and she really likes a particular boy in her year at school. She has heard that he likes her too and he has been sending her some sexualised text messages that she hasn't shown to anyone. Emily feels a bit uncomfortable about the idea of the messages being about sex but she really likes this boy and doesn't want him to stop making contact with her. She thinks she may have to start sexting if she wants him to stay interested. She is a little bit excited about the fact that he is interested in her in that way because she really fancies him too. But she is worried that if she starts to write messages that are about sex then he might put pressure on her to meet him and do these sexual things. She doesn't feel ready for any real sex yet at all.

Let's look at Emily's feelings and thoughts one by one.

Emily's Feelings

- Confusion (about what to do)
- Excited (that this boy likes her and finds her attractive)
- Confident (because this boy finds her attractive)
- Worried (because if she doesn't sext he might lose interest in her)
- Anxious (because if she does sext he may show his friends and everyone will find out or he may expect her to have sex)
- Distracted (she likes this boy so much, she can hardly focus on school work)

Emily's Thoughts

- I don't know what to do.
- If I don't sext him he will lose interest, and if I do everyone will probably know and I don't want that.
- I don't feel comfortable at all with this.
- I feel more confident because he finds me attractive and that feels really good.
- I wish I could concentrate on other things.

- I wish I knew what to do.
- I don't know if I can trust him.
- I definitely don't want to have sex.

Above all, Emily is extremely confused.

There is an opportunity here to explain that confusion can be felt when there are a lot of different thoughts going on and sometimes the thoughts can feel very jumbled up. You can suggest to your child that if Emily was to write out her feelings and thoughts it would start her on a path towards less confusion. (While young people may not actually follow through and do this when they are feeling confused, they at least have the option and know it is something that can help.)

You can write out Emily's thoughts for your child to see. Matching each thought then with a feeling is a good opportunity to highlight the link between feelings and thoughts.

The Link between Thoughts and Belief

Beliefs inform and impact hugely how a person thinks. Any one of Emily's thoughts can be focused on in order to explore what her beliefs might be. Here are three examples of links between thoughts and the beliefs that could be informing them:

Thought One

- *If I don't sext him he will lose interest.*

Focusing on this thought is an opportunity for you to look at what Emily believes about herself with your child.

Belief about Self

This thought – 'If I don't sext him, he will lose interest' – is one that is causing a difficult feeling for Emily. She doesn't want the boy to lose interest but doesn't feel ok about sending a sext either because of where it might lead. It is helpful for Emily to look at her beliefs about herself as this will help clarify where this thought is coming from. Thoughts are not facts but they sometimes can seem like facts if you think them enough. In this case, Emily thinking the boy may lose interest may, in her own mind, turn into an actual fact.

In order to start looking at her beliefs about herself, Emily needs to ask herself:

- What do I think about myself; am I worthy of respect and good care?
- What do I believe about how others should treat me?
- Do I believe that I should be in charge of my own behaviour and that if I make a choice then this should be accepted by my peers?
- Do I believe I have to act in a particular way in order for people to like me?

These questions are good ones for Emily to ask herself in order to work out her self-belief. You can suggest to your child that they should think about how *they* might answer these questions. They may or may not be willing to discuss this with you but you could write out the questions for them so that they could think about it when they are by themselves. If Emily believes that she is worthy of respect and good care, and that her behaviour choices should be accepted by peers, she may start to think in the following way (which will lower her level of confusion):

- If I decide not to sext this boy I could still text and tell him that I like him. If he is a nice person, then he will accept that I don't want to send a sext.
- He might like me even more if he thinks I'm strong enough to say no.
- He may see me as more attractive because confidence is attractive. And if he doesn't, then maybe he's not my kind of person.

As you go through this case study with your child, you can explain how self-belief plays a part in the outcome or the decision made. The purpose of this exercise is not to try to influence any future decisions your child will make (as they will make their own decisions anyway) but rather it is to give them the skills to work through how they can manage difficult feelings. That is the main focus of this exercise.

(Although it's always acceptable and useful to let your child know what you believe is the right thing to do and why you think that.)

Thought Two

- *I don't feel comfortable at all with this.*

Focusing on this thought provides an opportunity for parents to introduce their child to the idea of objectification. Objectification is the seeing or treating of a person as an object. Objectification is something all young people should be aware of and develop an opinion about.

Belief about Objectification

While there can be different causes of discomfort, in Emily's case it is probably tied in to her feeling:

- Not at all ready for sexting, especially with someone she hardly knows or
- Not comfortable with the idea of possibly being viewed in a sexual way or like a sexual object by someone

Young people will understand what you mean when they say that maybe Emily doesn't feel ready for something but they are less likely to understand what is meant by objectification. You can emphasise again how important beliefs are when it comes to thoughts. And even when beliefs are not consciously known, they can still be there and have influence, such as a possible belief that Emily holds about objectification.

It is probable that a young person in early adolescence or younger may not yet have heard of the term 'objectification'. Therefore, it is safe to assume that they do not yet have a belief formed about the issue. This issue was explored in Chapter 1. But to briefly reiterate, in this discussion the main thing is to begin by explaining that objectification means seeing or treating someone like an object. Take the example of Emily. If the boy she is in contact with sees her just as an object, for example, a pretty face and breasts, and doesn't see that she is a person with real feelings and real personality then it is possible that he is objectifying her. Ask your child if they think it would be ok to be treated like an object. The conversation can include a reference to the fact that everyone has different ideas about objectification; some people think it's ok and some people think it is absolutely not ok. Some people may even wish to be objectified because if they are seen as a sexual object it can give them something to cling on to as a sign of their worth. You can ask your son or daughter what they think about that: the idea that being objectified can make some people feel good, that a person would source their confidence based on feedback about their sexual attractiveness. You can point out that because objectifying others is common in the world today some young people start to do this without even being aware that they are doing it. It only becomes a real choice once you understand what it is.

If your child develops their own opinion on objectification this gives them power over their own mind and they are less likely then to be so gullible when it comes to messages they inadvertently get through media and social media. Young people generally don't have to have a clear belief about objectification as their beliefs about many things are still developing but they will benefit greatly from having an awareness about the fact that objectification can and does happen. And it happens frequently on social media and with selfies. Having awareness about objectification is very helpful for young people in many ways. It helps to protect them from behaviours such as:

- Sending sexually explicit images of themselves as a way to feel of worth
- Requesting sexual content from others and objectifying the person
- Accessing sexually explicit content posted by others, or accessing pornography (the viewing of which involves objectification)

One of the main differences between a person and an object is that a person has feelings and an object does not. At a very basic level, this is something that needs to be taught to young people. By objectifying others, even unintentionally, people can get to a point where they genuinely forget that the person behind the image is real, with real emotions. And if people lose sight of this, they can act in a disrespectful way towards others.

Emily's thought is that she does not feel comfortable with feeling pressure to send a sext. She doesn't want the boy to lose interest in her but she doesn't want to send a sext just to keep him happy either. Looking at her belief about objectification, Emily can work out to some extent what she wants to do. She can ask herself the following questions:

- Do I believe that if I send a sext he will start to see me as an 'object' for him to just look at?
- Do I believe that I am more than an object and deserve to be seen as more than an object?
- Do I believe that sending a sext to someone who hasn't really had a chance to get to know me well gives them the idea that it's ok to treat me like an object?

These kinds of questions may be difficult and strange for young people to consider, as it is not normal behaviour for young people to examine their beliefs about objectification.

Just because objectification on social media is extremely common it does not mean that it is something that is healthy or ok. If you want to prepare your child to manage well on social media, your child needs to learn how to examine their beliefs. With guidance and support, your child can learn to do this.

If Emily does not wish to send a sext because she believes she might be treated like an object if she sends one, she also needs to feel strong enough within herself to follow through with what she thinks is right for her. Peer pressure can be tough and it is important that Emily has a belief in herself such as 'If I do what is right for me, other people will just have to respect that' in order to make the decision. Her belief about objectification is only part of what will influence her behaviour. Many young people feel that sending a sext does not feel right, but they send them anyway as they feel peer pressure building.

Thought Three

- *I feel more confident because he finds me attractive and that feels really good.*

Focusing on this thought provides an opportunity to explore Emily's belief about how much the way you look relates to how much 'worth' you feel.

Beliefs about Worth

Everyone has a belief about their worth, even if that belief is buried deep. Having a high level of self-worth is good for young people as it makes them less likely to compromise themselves in order to be liked by others. It means also that the young person is less likely to depend on feedback from others in order to feel good about themselves.

For young girls and boys going onto social media today, the ideas dominant in society about the importance of appearance (particularly for females) is hard to ignore. Because ideas about the value of being 'sexy' or 'attractive' are so pervasive, it is important that your child, when going online, has the opportunity to think through and decide for themselves what it is they wish to believe about how important these things are.

Most people would agree that it feels good to feel attractive but if your child holds rigidly to a belief about their own worth, or a belief about the importance of appearance, there can be consequences for them, such as:

- They can become narcissistic and self-absorbed, spending hours editing selfies.
- They can develop an obsession with their appearance.
- They can become anxious and depressed because of how they look.

Your child is growing up in the age of the selfie culture. So they need to be supported to take a step back and think about how they want to position themselves and their worth within this culture. They will benefit from doing this, and it will impact on how they engage with others online.

The Impact of Tying Self-Worth to Appearance

If your child believes that being perceived as 'sexy' or 'sexually attractive' means they are of greater 'worth', one of two things could happen. In the case of a girl like Emily, she could engage in sexting or become obsessed with posting sexual selfies just to maintain this feeling of being of 'high worth', and if she engages in sexting she could start to feel under pressure to have sexual contact with this boy. The second thing that can happen is that not being sexually pursued could cause a young person to begin to feel 'worth-less'. Feeling you are worth less than someone who is deemed sexy (and worth more) can lead to a feeling of worthlessness. This feeling of worthlessness can be a factor in the development of all sorts of mental health difficulties for young people, such as anxiety, depression, self-harming behaviours and eating disorders.

Here are some questions to ask your child to prompt an exploration of their own developing beliefs about the links between appearance, attractiveness and a person's worth:

Questions to prompt exploring the beliefs of a boy:

- What do you think of Emily's thought, 'I feel more confident because he finds me attractive'?
- Do you think she sees herself as worth more because she is attractive to this person?
- It seems to give her more confidence. Do you think that's a good thing to rely on for confidence?
- Do girls you know seem more confident or less confident depending on how they look?
- Why do you think that is?
- Do you think it's ok for girls to feel pressure to look a certain way? What about for boys?
- What do you think it's like for girls to have to deal with this pressure? Do boys deal with it too?
- What way do you think about a person's 'worth'?
- Do you rate a person's 'worth' based on their appearance?
- What about your own 'worth'?

Questions to prompt exploring the beliefs of a girl:

- What do you think of Emily's thought, 'I feel more confident because he finds me attractive'?
- Do you think she sees herself as 'worth more' because this boy finds her attractive?
- It seems to give her more confidence; do you think that's a good thing to rely on for confidence?

- How much does attractiveness matter to girls, do you think?
- How much does it matter to you?
- Do you think people make a choice about how they define their own 'worth' or are people just going along with what seems to be normal?
- Do you think that the pressure on girls to look a certain way might be to do with industries making money out of people feeling they need to buy make-up, etc.? Do you think boys feel similar pressure?
- Do you think a person's 'worth' is much more complex than how a person looks? Do you think it's shallow?
- Is it like objectification, do you think?

It is good to connect back to the possible consequences of Emily's action if she does decide to send a sext. Questions such as these can help:

- Do you think if Emily sent the sext she would feel pressure to engage in sexual stuff? (You can add that sometimes people do.)
- Do you think Emily would worry about other people seeing it? (You can add that once a person sends a picture, they can't be in charge of where it goes or who gets to view it.)
- Do you think Emily would feel proud of herself if she decided to wait until she felt ready before sending any sexts to anyone, if that's what felt right for her?

THE LINK BETWEEN FEELINGS, THOUGHTS AND BELIEFS

Beliefs influence thoughts. Thoughts influence feelings. And feelings influence behaviour. It is important that your child knows this link. Then they can practice:

- Recognising and naming the feeling, then
- Being able to identify what they are thinking, then
- Being able to see what beliefs are influencing them to think that way

This is a straightforward way to manage difficult emotions such as confusion, anger and anxiety. Even if the feeling is large, such as a strong angry feeling, if your child knows how to pause, recognise the angry feeling, recognise and name the thoughts, and then work out the belief that is influencing that thought, they are much less likely to post something impulsively from a place of anger that could lead them down a path where they could fall out with a friend or be accused of cyber-bullying. It is essential that your child knows how to pause and work through difficult feelings. It increases the chances of them and others in their social media world being safe.

Being able to put a limit on social media use, taking regular breaks from it, is a very good habit to develop. It gives young people space to focus on what they might be feeling without being constantly bombarded with content. When young people are constantly plugged in on social media they are not getting the chance to work through and think about how the content is impacting on them. Regular breaks are very helpful and necessary and should be built into your child's social media habits from the start. Breaks from social media are very important and not just as a way to be able to manage difficult emotions. In terms of managing stress, managing a good sleep routine and being able to concentrate fully on whatever it is your child is engaged in doing, putting some limit on the time they are spending on social media is important. This may translate into no social media use after a certain time in the evening and/or no social media during homework or meal times.

It can also be helpful to have regular conversations with your child about the benefit of not spending too much time online, as they could then be missing out on other experiences in the real (rather than the virtual) world. By making rules from the start about times that social media and internet access is switched off in the home, it is more likely that your child will follow through with the rules and comply. Consistency and following through matters a lot when it comes to the setting of limits. And parents need to try to lead by example on this issue too by also having limits on their own social media use when around their children. There is no more powerful influence than a parent who not just talks the talk but who also is willing to walk the walk!

5

STEP FIVE: HOW TO RECOVER IF THINGS GO WRONG

'Nobody can go back and start a new beginning, but anyone can start today and make a new ending.'

Maria Robinson, author

THE IMPORTANCE OF BEING PREPARED

While it is not inevitable that something will 'go wrong' on social media, it's best not to assume that everything will definitely go right either. Things can go wrong for anyone. All sorts of things are influencing what happens to young people online and parents are sometimes really shocked that, despite their efforts, something totally unexpected and out of the blue happens to their child. Even if your child:

- Knows about psychological development
- Knows how to source confidence internally
- Has secure attachment
- Knows how to manage their feelings

something can still go wrong. That's just how life is. And so while you don't want your child to be on high alert for danger all the time, it is worthwhile reminding them of the simple fact that sometimes things do go wrong. Working through the case studies in this book is a way to equip your child to manage if things go wrong for them. Or it can even be a way to minimise the chances that things do go wrong as information is power.

It is important to think ahead and to consider and plan for the possibility of tough times. The purpose of doing this is not to evoke any feelings of panic or anxiety. You already know that things can sometimes go wrong, even if we'd sometimes prefer to keep our heads in the sand about it. Thinking ahead about recovery places you and your child in a more powerful position in relation to any issue that they may have to face. Thinking ahead will help build resilience for your child and this will help them cope better if tough times come their way.

INFLUENCING RECOVERY – WHAT HELPS?

When it comes to young people recovering from a traumatic incident or general upset, the attachment and relationship between them and their parent(s) comes into play. If your child is going through a tough time you may or may not know about it. Having a secure attachment relationship makes it more likely that your child will talk to you and feel they can lean on you for support (although other factors influence this too). During adolescence, and particularly as adolescence goes on, young people start to shift from having their main attachment with their parent(s) to it being to somebody else. This could be a close friend, a girlfriend/boyfriend or someone else. One of the things that can be hard (and it can be hard at any age) is if this main attachment relationship breaks down. If this relationship was providing a secure base, it is important that you can step into the space left so that your child still has a secure base. As your child gets older and goes into the late teenage years, you can chat with them about who they have to lean on for support. It is important to let them know they can talk to you about absolutely anything at all that might be happening.

It can be very difficult for a young person who has developed a relationship with someone to suddenly have their secure base disappear. Because the main attachment a younger adolescent has is still usually to a parent, while at the same time they are starting to transition away from parents as their secure base provider, it can be tricky for young people in crisis to know who they should lean on for support.

Another point to consider is that even if attachment is secure the particular emotion being felt by the young person can cause a block to them opening up and communicating. The young person may feel fear or embarrassment or shame in relation to what is happening to them and they may not have full self-awareness about what a difficult time they are having. They may even be beginning to feel numb, as an unconscious self-protective process takes hold to block out the pain of what they are going through and so it can be really hard to even know what to say to a parent. It is important therefore that you keep the lines of communication open with your child and that the feelings of shame, embarrassment and fear are normalised. For example, if your child is aware of fights being organised through social media where people are getting badly hurt and they fear they may get hurt too the fear of the repercussions of telling an adult may act as a barrier to them opening up. It is important to reassure them that if fear is stopping them telling you something that they can tell you anyway and you will find a way to help them. An example of how parents can do this is to say something like the following:

'You know it's normal to feel all sorts of emotions, including fear, embarrassment or shame. I have felt these feelings and maybe you will too. I want you to remember that they are all normal things to feel. And don't ever think that if you feel those feelings that you cannot talk to me about something that is going on. The most important thing for me is that you feel ok and that you feel able to talk to me about absolutely anything. And I want you to come to me if things are ever not ok, even if you feel embarrassed, afraid or ashamed. Or if you begin to feel numb, tell me that too. If it is too hard to talk to me ever, or if you can't work out how you feel, write me a note and hand it to me. I promise I will help find a way to support you if times get tough. Don't let worry or fear of the consequences of telling me hold you back. You can tell me anything and I will support you.'

I have met young people who have had to deal with traumatic events and some find it very hard to open up to their parents even though their parents wish they would, but we should never underestimate the power of secure attachment. Hostility and lack of compassion are two things that undermine secure attachment. Holding onto this knowledge as kids grow is one massively positive thing that you can do to support your child.

WHAT IF PROFESSIONAL HELP IS REQUIRED WHEN SOMETHING GOES WRONG?

Sometimes, when young people are going through a tough time because of something that has happened online, professional help is required. A visit to a GP is a good first step to take as they can discuss the possible options around therapeutic support. If psychotherapy is required, it is important to ensure that the psychotherapist chosen is accredited with a professional organisation. That way, you can ensure a high standard of care for your child. It is also good for young people to know of services online that can help support their mental health; check if your child does. SpunOut.ie, teenlineIreland.ie, teenlineonline.org and mental-health.org.uk are good online services to be aware of.

WHAT CAN GO WRONG ON SOCIAL MEDIA?

Many different situations can occur that cause young people not to feel ok. Here are three general types of situations:

- A situation involving potential danger involving some action the child has taken themselves.
- A situation where someone else (not the child) does or says something that causes difficulty for the child.
- A situation where the difficulty lies within the child's mind, in their thoughts and beliefs.

Below are some fictional case studies that we can use to examine the process of what can happen in each of these types of situations.

CASE STUDY ONE: A SITUATION INVOLVING POTENTIAL DANGER FOR YOUR CHILD

MOLLY'S STORY

Molly is fifteen years old and lives at home with her mum, dad and three older brothers. They are a family of high achievers; two of her brothers are already in college and her other brother is working hard to get into college later this year. Molly always liked school. She is good at her work and, in the main, finds most subjects easy. She has a nice group of friends who also enjoy school and work hard. They go to each other's houses sometimes and at the weekend they like to go to the cinema. Molly has been on social media for a few years now. It has never really caused her any problems and she enjoys connecting with her friends on it. Molly knows girls in her school have been bullied online but nothing like that ever happened to her. Everyone just seems to leave her be.

Molly knows that some girls in her class send sexy pictures to boys in her year. They also use Yellow, an app that lets you 'hook up' with people locally whom you like. Molly doesn't want to use that app though as she feels the boys might reject her. She also heard that one girl ended up being forced to do something to a boy she met on that app as he said that because she met him through Yellow she must have been 'keen' to perform sexual acts. She hears quite a lot about sexual stuff that goes on at her local disco but she's never involved in any of it and people don't seem to expect her to get involved. She's seen as a 'good girl who studies', who wouldn't do stuff like that. She has never even kissed a boy but what others don't realise is that she would love a boy to kiss her.

No boys in her class have ever asked her for a sexy picture, even though she sometimes wonders what it would be like if they did. She knows her group of friends are viewed as the 'brainy' girls who love books and study but she is curious about other stuff too, like boys. Her friends don't ever talk about sex stuff or kissing boys and her parents don't talk to her about it either. Molly has heard a few other girls in her class talk about a social media site, like Facebook, which people use if they are interested in sex. She knows this site is for adults and is called Fuckbook and she is pretty sure her parents would not have heard of it. Molly decides to check out Fuckbook, just to see what it is like. She is curious, nervous and a little bit excited by the prospect. She decides not to tell anyone as she just wants to have a look herself. She is sure no one will find out what she is doing because her parents trust her and hardly ever check her phone and she thinks there is no way any of her friends would be on Fuckbook so she'll be able to check it out in secret.

In order to check it out, Molly has to lie about her age as it stipulates you need to be an adult to use the site. She sets up a fake profile and adds a picture but makes sure it's quite dark so no one can really properly see her face. She thinks that it'll be ok, as she only intends to have a look. As soon as she does this, Molly gets a compliment from a boy on the site who thinks her picture is really lovely. Molly didn't put her full face in the picture as she knows not to, but the picture did have her smile and that's what he complimented her on. Molly says thank you; she has always been polite and she is flattered. The boy looks to be her age and Molly thinks he probably put up a fake age too. Molly wonders if this boy is a bit like her, in a group of friends where sex and kissing are not talked about but curious to see what it's all about.

Four weeks later, Molly is beginning to lose sleep. The boy has started messaging her constantly. While at first it was just to ask her how her day was going, he is now sending her explicit messages and images and expecting her to do the same. It's beginning to dawn on Molly that he's a lot older than he said he was. She doesn't know what to do or who she can tell. Now that she has a profile on the site, she feels stuck. Not only is she not sleeping properly, she is finding it hard to concentrate in school. She hasn't told anyone at all what she has been doing. She is pretty sure her parents know something is up but she thinks they would be completely horrified and mad if they knew what she had been doing. She thinks:

- How can I possibly tell them I was curious about sex and that this boy now wants to meet me?
- Maybe if I tell him I don't want anything to do with him, he will just leave me alone.

Molly is in a difficult situation and the stress is rising. She goes into school and starts to have a panic attack.

Looking at the Context

Any young person can get themselves into a difficult situation where danger would be apparent to an adult but not necessarily to them. This is particularly true where social media is concerned. The lines between social media and pornography are blurring. People are uploading home-made videos and photos onto porn sites and the porn industry is not vigilant in checking if people featured in the videos have given consent before the content is uploaded. As well as this, images from social media sites are being stolen and uploaded onto porn sites. This is called revenge porn and young people need to be aware of the dangers of it. Images given to a sexual partner can be uploaded to a porn site or specific revenge porn site if the relationship ends. Sometimes the explicit images are accompanied by identifying information such as the subject's name, address or social media handles, which is extremely dangerous and exploitative. For young people caught up in this type of danger, where they are exposed or a threat of exposure is made, it can be challenging to talk about it with a parent. So, as a parent, you need to explicitly tell your child that this kind of thing can happen. Name the risks. Your child needs to be aware that they cannot assume that they can trust someone to be who they say they are and the age they say they are (this is something some adults still don't fully grasp and adults can get caught up in difficult situations too). If you are speaking to or interacting with someone online, it is not safe to assume automatically that the person is telling the truth. Hard as that is to stomach, it is necessary for young people to be informed. They are naturally more trusting and more gullible than adults and so, as parents, we need to lead them towards safe behaviours. In this case, it is clear that Molly's behaviour is far from safe.

Age Restrictions

One good way for you to try to prevent this type of situation occurring is to take a very strong position from the very start on age restrictions and the necessity of them. This would mean only letting young people access social media sites that are age appropriate; if they are eleven, don't let them on a social media site that is deemed suitable for age thirteen. If her parents had make it clear from the very outset that she was only allowed access to sites that are deemed suitable for her age, because that is what is considered safe, then Molly, in this situation, would have been more likely to know that going onto this site was potentially very unsafe. Conversations about safety need to happen at a young age and they need to continue as time goes by. Another thing you can do right from the start is to download protective software so that adult-only sites are blocked and out of the reach of adolescents.

Spotting Dangers Ahead of Time

Young people need to be prepared ahead of time to spot danger like this and accessing sites that are not for their age group is obviously risky. While taking a strong position on age restrictions has consequences when children are at a younger age (as it would mean children under thirteen would not be allowed access to Facebook, Snapchat, etc.), it is still a valid position as it is part of what creates a safe environment for young people as they grow up. Part of being a teenager involves pushing and testing boundaries. And so parenting around social media means you need to stay one step ahead.

While you may not wish to alert your child to the existence of sites such as these, it is important that you, at least, are aware that these sites exist. Sites such as Fuckbook (a porn version of Facebook), PornTube (a porn version of YouTube) and Pornostagram (a porn version of Instagram) exist and could very well be a site your child is hearing about in school. To bring up the issue of pornography and dangerous social media sites with your teenager, you can talk about what sites they are accessing and how they decide if the site they are on is safe or not. In relation to porn, you should emphasise to your teens that porn is not what real sex is like and that porn teaches people nothing about the issue of consent.

Conversations about porn and social media and the uploading of sexualised content can form part of the conversation about the existence of sites that are not at all safe. You don't even have to name the sites if you don't want to, but the issue of unsafe sites needs to be addressed. By addressing it, you will give your child some important messages such as:

- I can talk about porn.
- I am willing to listen.

- I am fully aware that these sites exist.
- I am absolutely open to discussing all topics of a sexual nature.

You need to be aware of the name of every social media site your child is using and I would suggest that be the way until they are eighteen. Social media sites such as Facebook, Snapchat and Instagram have a minimum age requirement of thirteen years. Parents often allow children younger than this age to use these sites and while it is up to each parent to decide what is best for their child, it is important to remember that no matter how bright or well-behaved a young person is, they can sometimes be naive to danger and get themselves into situations that they then don't know how to get out of, like Molly. Don't take the chance.

Molly's Curiosity about Sex

While some young people like Molly may seem to show little or no interest in sex or relationships, it is still good for them to have the opportunity to get proper information and to talk about their feelings about sex and pornography at home. You can normalise the feeling of embarrassment or discomfort that a child like Molly may feel by saying that it's ok to feel that way and that the more they talk, the easier it will become. Another option in a situation like this one is to suggest to your child that if there is something they want to talk about but they don't know how to, they can frame it as being about a 'friend'. For example, 'My friend is after getting themselves into a particular situation and they don't know what to do' or 'My friend would love if boys showed interest in her but they don't and she doesn't know what to do.'

If you say to your child ahead of time that it is ok to talk about something in that way, both as a way to get the talking started and as a way to get support, it is possible that they will feel they have another option in terms of getting the talking started. They may find it easier to open up initially as the conversation will feel less personal. If the conversation does happen about 'a friend', then it is important for you to say that even if it was a story about something that was happening to them, rather than it being about their friend, you would want to help them feel ok and you would support them. You can reiterate the message that you will listen to or talk about anything at all, even if it is something that makes them feel fear, shame, guilt or embarrassment.

What Parents Can Do to Help Recovery: Molly's Story

Molly's parents are tuned in enough to notice that she seems tired in the mornings and she is more irritable than normal. They have noticed her spending more time alone while in the house; this is a change as she used to be happy to spend at least some of her evening with the rest of the family. Molly's parents decide to talk to her about how she is feeling. But then the school phones them to say that Molly has had a panic attack. They are shocked and worried and collect Molly early from school. They tell Molly that she can tell them what is going on. They tell her that she can write out what she is feeling and what she is thinking as a way to get started with working out what to do. They reassure her that the panic is a sign of very high stress and that having one panic attack does not mean that she is going to have another.

(Note: experiencing a panic attack can sometimes in and of itself cause more panic so it is good for young people to know that one panic attack does not have to lead to more. That way, they will hopefully, at the very least, not panic about the panic.)

Her parents tell Molly that they need to work out what is going on in her head and that it is important for her to feel she can trust them to help her. They tell her they want her to trust them and they set a time aside for later that day to talk to her. They speak to her gently and with an emphasis on how important it is that she feels she can talk to them about anything, even if she feels shame, guilt, fear or embarrassment. (These are the feelings that can block communication so it's good to name them.) They normalise these feelings, saying that everyone, even they, feel these things at times. They ask Molly to talk to them or to write them a note. They tell her that it will all be ok. And they reassure her that they love her.

What Happens if Molly Doesn't Open Up?

If Molly doesn't open up, her parents can go to the GP to seek advice. The GP may be able to speak to Molly or refer her on to a mental health professional, if this is warranted. It is not always possible for parents to get young people to open up to them but by specifically tailoring your support in the way Molly's parents did above (emphasising the link between her feeling of panic and her thoughts; not being hostile and showing compassion; reassuring her) it is more likely that your child will open up and trust you.

What if Molly Does Tell Them What Is Going On?

In a situation such as the one Molly finds herself in, a number of things need to happen if Molly opens up. They are:

- Molly needs reassurance that she did the right thing by opening up to her parents. Her parents need to tell her very clearly that they are really glad that she decided to tell them and trust them with her difficult and dangerous situation. This will create a positive context and will aid Molly in deciding she could talk to her parents again, if she ever has anything further to reveal in the future.
- Molly needs to be supported to work through and name what she is feeling.
- Molly then needs to be supported to identify what she is thinking and also what she was thinking as her online relationship with this boy/older man developed online. During this process, her parents need to be careful to focus on Molly's emotions and thoughts and keep a check on their own reactions and feelings. Molly will likely need a total break from social media until she has worked out how to keep safe. A conversation about pornography and the blurred lines between porn and social media is absolutely essential as part of the discussion on keeping safe in future.
- Molly needs to look at her beliefs about herself and her confidence sources. This does not need to be done at the point of disclosure to her parents. But it needs to happen at some point so her parents could set aside time later in the week to look at this issue.

A safety plan needs to be put in place for Molly. This would include:

- Taking Molly's profile off the site
- Increasing the level of monitoring that is taking place so Molly can no longer access sites that are not for her age group
- Educating Molly about engaging with people online whom she does not know
- Educating Molly about the danger of posting any information online about herself that she would not like made public
- Educating Molly about pornography and how to handle the fact that so much sexually explicit material is available online
- Educating Molly about consent

Support for Parents

If this kind of situation arises, parents can put all their energy into helping their child recover but then can become distraught and also paranoid about the potential dangers for their child going forward, or the potential danger for their other children. Once you are aware of the need to monitor and tune into your children's online activity there is less danger for them but it is worthwhile to consider seeking support for yourself when an incident like this occurs. When you have to support your child recover from a difficult and dangerous incident online it is absolutely valid to consider what support you as a parent now need for yourself.

CASE STUDY TWO: WHEN SOMEONE ELSE'S WORDS OR ACTIONS CAUSE DIFFICULTY FOR YOUR CHILD

EUGENE'S STORY

Eugene and Paul are thirteen years old and are in the same class in school. They have been friends since they were both five years old. They enjoy sport and are on the same football team. Eugene is starting to notice that Paul only talks to him in school if two other boys in his class, Matt and Kevin, are not around. Eugene doesn't like Matt and Kevin. He was on the same football team as them last year and he knows that while they are good fun to be around, they can be mean. Eugene is aware that they have made fun of him more than a few times and they have posted nasty comments about him on social media.

Eugene has a feeling that Paul is only using him to have someone to hang out with when Matt and Kevin are not around. Even though this is what he thinks, he is afraid to say anything to Paul, in case Paul tells the other boys, they laugh at him or Eugene gets a hard time in some other way for raising it.

One day Eugene goes into school and Paul ignores him completely. He later goes onto Facebook and sees that Paul has 'unfriended' him. Paul has blocked him on Snapchat too. Eugene can't understand what he has done to make Paul so suddenly and so completely reject him. He must have done something, he thinks, for Paul to treat him in this way. Eugene is so upset and feels as if he has no friends at all now. Paul has been his best friend for so long and he was closer to him than he ever was to anyone else in school. He thinks Paul must want to give him a very clear message, to stay well away from him and out of his life.

Eugene thinks:

- How awkward is school going to be?
- How can I even face it?

Eugene starts to imagine what it would be like not to have to go to school. He imagines not having to face Paul or anyone else in the class. He starts to imagine how good it would feel to just simply disappear and not have to deal with this messiness. He wonders if anyone would even care if he did disappear. 'Maybe', he thinks, 'Paul would care then. Maybe he'd feel bad then.'

How Others Behave Online and in Real Life

In this situation, there is a similarity between how Paul acted towards Eugene online and in real life. It is sometimes the case that people act differently online than they do in person. It is good to talk to your child about the possibility of dealing with this difference, as it can be difficult for them to work out what is going on.

Because Paul is behaving the same on and offline, it is easier for Eugene to work out 'a version of truth' about what is going on. Paul seems to be telling him, without saying it directly, that he wants Eugene out of his life. This might be for now or it could be that he wants him out forever, and so, understandably, Eugene feels hurt. How Eugene interprets Paul's actions are of critical importance to his recovery from this. His interpretation of Paul's actions will be influenced by a number of factors. By discussing each of these factors in turn with your child you are teaching them to pause and assess how they process their own interpretations of events and so this will help to keep them safe.

What Factors Influence How Eugene Interprets and Deals with this Situation?

A number of factors impact and influence how Eugene interprets and deals with this situation and also how he recovers:

- Does he tune into how he is feeling and then link his feeling to what he is thinking?
- Does he know how what he believes may be influencing his thinking?
- Is he thinking in a concrete rather than an abstract way?
- Does he know about the psychological task of identity formation and how this may be a way to understand why Paul is being so mean?
- Does he have a secure base and is he aware of how this can help him?
- Is his source of confidence mostly internal or mostly external?
- Does he understand how confidence can be affected sometimes, when things happen that are outside a person's control? Does he know how to mind his confidence so it does not spill out?

Tuning in to a Feeling and Matching the Feeling with a Thought

For a young person feeling as Eugene does, this step – of tuning into how he is feeling – is extremely important. Why?

If he feels really low and does not pay attention to that, the feeling could influence his behaviour in a way that could lead him to harm himself (if he starts to feel hopeless, for example). Eugene (or any young person in a similar situation) may have been dealing with this issue with

Paul (or any friend or peer) being mean to him for some time. In the case study Eugene has noticed that Paul only seems to talk to him when the other two boys are not around. Therefore Eugene may have been experiencing hurt and worry or annoyance about this for some time and his thoughts about it may have become quite set in stone. When Eugene was completely ignored by Paul in school, he may have felt a mix of:

- Hurt
- Sadness
- Embarrassment
- Anxiety
- Anger

And then when he saw he was unfriended online, it is possible he felt these things even more and he may also have felt despair. Despair is a particularly risky feeling as it means there is a lack of hope. If despair is felt and it is not addressed negative outcomes can result. It is the complete absence of hope that increases the risk of self-harm and young people need to know that tuning into emotion includes checking in with themselves to make sure they are not coming close to feeling despair. If they are and it seems to be ongoing, it may be time to consider accessing professional support.

Eugene could become very low if he does not tune in to how he is feeling and if he does not know how to take action to mind himself. One action he can take is to match the way he is feeling to his thoughts. Here is an example of what could result from that:

Feeling	Thoughts
Hurt	I can't believe Paul would do this to me.
Sadness	Paul doesn't care about me.
Embarrassment	Everyone in class will think I'm a loser.
Anxiety	I don't know what to do. I can't sort this out.
Anger	This is not fair; I don't get to be in control of this.

Understanding How Beliefs Can Impact on Thoughts

When Eugene has identified his thoughts he can then look at what he believes and how that is influencing his thoughts. It is worth working through this example with your child so they know about the steps involved in recovering from a difficult incident.

Eugene may believe that friends are not meant to treat each other this way, that he doesn't deserve to be treated this way, and these are helpful beliefs to have. But he also may believe that he is less worthy of a good friend than others, that he won't be able to sort this situation out, that things will never improve or that he will never be able to have a friend again.

It is vital that young people who may face this type of situation know how to tune into what they are feeling, what they are thinking and what they believe. What they believe about themselves, the future and the consequences of this having happened to them in the first place all matter. If their beliefs are mostly negative, such as 'Things are awful and never will get better again', it can be very risky if this is not identified as a belief. That is because beliefs influence thoughts which influence feelings which influence behaviours. Beliefs if left unchallenged can begin to feel like facts.

Self-harm is one behaviour that can be engaged in if young people feel very low and in despair. Teaching your child how to cope with this type of situation by going through Eugene's thoughts, feelings and beliefs with them makes it possible for them to then mind themselves better in a similar situation.

Concrete Versus Abstract Thinking

Moving from a concrete (black-and-white) way of thinking to a more abstract (nuanced) way of thinking is part of the process of growing through adolescence. So for all young people they are some way along this journey; perhaps if they are Eugene's age of thirteen years, they are at the very beginning of it. In Eugene's example, it is important to point out to your child how seeing things in a black-and-white way can do Eugene a disservice as he only has one perspective to view things from. If his perspective is negative about himself, this will make him feel bad about himself. For example, he may tend to see things in this way:

- Paul doesn't like me anymore; no one likes me.

Abstract thinking would allow for two or more possible ideas about what is going on:

- Maybe Paul does not like me anymore *or*
- Maybe Paul is just trying to get in with these new guys and doesn't want them to get to know me in case they like me more than him.

If Eugene can think in an abstract way or discuss how he feels and thinks with someone who can think in an abstract way he will have better options in terms of managing how he feels and then how to react. Therefore, opening up to someone you trust not just about how you feel but about how you are thinking too will be helpful.

How Identity Formation Helps Explain Paul's Behaviour

It is extremely difficult for young people like Eugene to deal with this sort of treatment online, and in Eugene's case it is treatment from someone whom he saw as a very close friend. While understanding the psychological task of adolescence, identity formation, will not take away the difficult feelings that Eugene may face, it can make it easier to bear because at least the behaviour can be understood in a particular context.

Understanding what might be going on for Paul from the point of view of psychological development gives a context for his behaviour and makes it less likely therefore that Eugene will see it as being just about him personally. Paul, like all young people, is dealing with the questions 'Who am I? What do others think of me?' in his unconscious mind. Because of this, Paul, like many young people, is moving between groups of friends and is drawn to new friends or peers in order to work out the answer to the question 'What do people think of me?' Paul may already know that Eugene likes him as they have been friends for a long time. Therefore, having Eugene as a friend is not helping him answer this question. Eugene gets effectively dumped by Paul but this could be because of Paul's psychological stage of development, rather than it being about Eugene not being a good friend or exciting or fun. Young people can start to think negatively about themselves if friends cut off contact with them. It is important for young people to realise that, in the main, this is more about the person doing the cutting off than it is to do with them. It is often not that the person no longer likes their friend, but rather, they want new people around so that they get new feedback about themselves. This is about psychological development.

The Importance of a Secure Base

Discussing the case study of Eugene with your child is a good opportunity to ask them what they would do in Eugene's situation and whether they would talk to someone they trust. Young people can have people in their world whom they trust but it might not dawn on them to turn to this person for support if the negative feeling builds quite quickly or if they begin to feel despair or hopelessness (as they would then think 'What's the point in talking?'). Part of what the young person can begin thinking and believing is that even talking to someone wouldn't help as nothing can help sort this situation out. You need to remind your children of the fact that you, as their parent(s), are there to listen and support, even during times when everything seems hopeless and a mess. There is always a way to recover. In this example, talking through how Eugene is feeling and thinking with a trusted adult could help in the following ways:

- Eugene may feel better by knowing someone really cares.
- Expressing how he feels is part of what helps him feel a little bit better.
- It can help him to work out what can be done, such as looking at the possible outcomes of saying something to Paul about what he has done.
- It can help Eugene look at what he can do to feel ok about going into school without losing confidence and without feeling anxious and self-conscious.
- It provides a safe haven to return to at the end of the school day. This can be something that helps as no matter how hard the day is, you know that someone else has you very much in mind as the day goes by.

Ask your child why else they think it might be useful for Eugene to talk to his parents. Ask them also what they think could happen if Eugene makes the choice not to talk to anyone at all about what has happened. Would they see a benefit and/or a negative consequence to this? Point out the danger of this, i.e. that Eugene could end up feeling very bad about himself and thinking no one cares. Make sure your child knows that Eugene's thoughts are not facts.

Internal Versus External Confidence

If you think back to the idea of confidence like water in a jug (Chapter 2), this situation with Eugene is one where the jug is at risk of being knocked over. Paul has treated Eugene badly and Eugene was not able to control that. It is important for Eugene to tune into what might be happening to his confidence as someone treating him the way Paul has done makes it likely that his confidence has been affected.

If water spills out of the jug – if a young person loses confidence – one thing they can do to prevent a major loss of confidence is to check how much of their confidence is coming from an internal source. If Eugene is able to talk to a parent about how he feels, his parent is in a good position to help Eugene work this out. The first step in this is for his parent to ask:

- How has this affected your confidence or has it?

Or you can ask your own child:

- Do you think this happening would affect Eugene's confidence?

Explain to your child that once Eugene has an internal source of confidence, he will be ok. In order to explain why this is, here is an example of what Eugene may feel:

> Eugene knows that Paul has treated him badly. He knows it is not something he would ever do to a friend as he is a kind and loyal person. Eugene also is aware of the fact that he treats people with respect and this is something he is proud of. He knows he is the type of person who stands up for others if that is what is needed. He doesn't understand why Paul has done what he has done but he has enough confidence (from knowing he is loyal, kind, respectful and a good friend) to know he deserves to be treated better than this. He decides to say something to Paul

> about what has happened. For example, he could say, 'I don't understand why you have cut me off but I do know that being treated that way is not what I deserve. If you want to talk about why you did it then I'll listen, but I want you to know that I know that I don't deserve to be treated in a disrespectful way.' Eugene also decides not to isolate himself from others in his social circle who are nice.

If Eugene thinks in this way, if he fills in his confidence circle in a way that focuses on the things about himself that are good and a potential source of confidence, it will help Eugene steady the jug.

If he doesn't do that, here is an example of what can happen:

> Eugene is not tuning in to what is good about himself. He is not tuning in to how he feels, what he thinks or what he believes. His confidence is spilling out and all he can think about is what the other boys and girls in his class will think of him when he goes back in there. He is so embarrassed. He can't face school. His confidence drops to such a low level that he unconsciously puts clingfilm over the top of the jug. He cuts himself off from others and starts spending more and more time alone in his room. He refuses to go to school.

So in this type of situation, if it was to occur, you can take the following steps to help aid your child's recovery:

- Give your child a chance to express how they are feeling. Give them space to express the hurt and sadness, if that's what they feel, and commend them on their ability to be honest in sharing their feelings with you.
- Check if they know how their feelings are linking to their thoughts as this will give them a sense of power over how they feel (once they have had time to lean in to the difficult and painful emotions).
- Talk to your child about the excluder dealing with the task of identity formation and perhaps needing different feedback from other peers (so that it's not felt so personally).

- Check to see how your child is interpreting the events and, if they are seeing it in a black-and-white way, support them to be less concrete in how they are thinking about it.
- Discuss your child's confidence, any spillage of water from their jug and brainstorm ways to gradually fill the water back up (mostly by thinking in a positive way about themselves).

Understanding How Confidence Can Be Impacted by the Actions of Others

When other people's actions cause hurt and anguish, it is really important that young people have a way of understanding how this can impact on their confidence. If this happens to your child, remind them of the jug analogy from Chapter 2. If they are aware of water being knocked out of their confidence jug, they can focus on keeping it steady. The way your child interprets an event won't necessarily stop them feeling sadness or hurt but being able to interpret an event in a way that keeps them feeling ok about themselves and ok about the future will help them recover from the incident.

Using the confidence circle (see Chapter 2) after an event such as Eugene's can be a way to give your child the message that there is always something that is within their control. We may not be able to control how others treat us but we can control how much we focus on minding ourselves and minding our mental health as the upset happens. Holding the jug steady is one way to mind ourselves. Once your child knows that, they are much more likely to recover from difficult incidents and return to feeling ok.

CASE STUDY THREE: WHEN THE DIFFICULTY LIES IN YOUR CHILD'S THOUGHTS AND BELIEFS

SOPHIE'S STORY

Sophie is sixteen years old. She has many friends and spends a lot of time on social media. She is popular in school with the boys. She enjoys being popular but suspects that the boys only like her because of her looks. Sophie and her friends spend a lot of time editing their selfies. They have fun posting them on Facebook and Instagram and she usually gets hundreds of likes for her selfie posts. If she doesn't get one hundred likes within an hour Sophie feels bad. She then starts to think about what might be wrong with her and she starts to wonder if she looks fat. Sophie follows a lot of celebrities on Instagram. She sees them getting so many likes and wishes that could be her life. The more she sees these celebrity selfies, the more she starts to think about what she can do to be like them. Her favourite celebrity is a social media star and Victoria's Secret model.

Sophie comes across a website about anorexia where people talk about their experience of losing weight and how they did it. She decides to follow some of the tips, just to see what happens. She starts to lose weight. Boys seem to like her even more as she loses weight and girls seem to be jealous. She is delighted, feels fantastic and really gets hooked on the idea of being desirable to them all and the 'skinny' one among her friends. She continues to limit her eating; her parents start to notice and get annoyed but Sophie doesn't care what they think. She thinks they wouldn't understand and she thinks they'll stop noticing as they are totally consumed with their business ventures.

Sophie's friends tell her they are concerned but Sophie thinks they are just jealous of the attention she is getting from the boys. She is feeling less energetic and starts to see her grades slip in school. She spends more time online comparing her weight to other people and she has no energy left to go out with her friends. She edits selfies and counts calories. Sophie is getting caught up in a spiral of self-destruction but it is hard for her to even see it. All she sees are the likes on her selfies and her number of followers increasing. That, for her, is becoming the thing that matters most.

Eating Disorders, Selfies and the World We Live in Today

The incidence of eating disorders has risen exponentially over the past number of decades. And while eating disorders are a very complex matter that do not always relate to a young person's belief about idealised body shapes, the selfie culture has well and truly placed a significant emphasis on physical appearance. Within teenage culture today, physical appearance, often digitally enhanced, has become a currency with which you 'buy' a sense of 'worth'. And while eating disorders are complex mental health disorders, we cannot ignore the fact that we now live in a world where there is intense focus given to body image, attractiveness and sex appeal. This incessant focus on appearance has impacted on notions people hold about worth and teenagers need to be given space to explore how this issue is impacting on their own sense of themselves.

What Eating Disorders Look Like

Eating disorders do not develop overnight and knowing some of the features of an eating disorder can be helpful for parents to know. Both boys and girls are affected by eating disorders such as anorexia. The disorder, once it takes hold, can involve:

- A fear of gaining weight
- Monitoring weight to the point of obsession
- Losing weight, once the disorder takes hold, becoming more important than anything else in the world

Someone who is developing an eating disorder like anorexia will likely also be developing a distorted body image as part of the disorder – a belief that their body shape is not ok. A distorted body image can (in part) be triggered by:

- Obsessively checking their number of selfie likes
- Obsessively altering their image/selfie in order to get more likes
- Constant monitoring of celebrity selfies and bodies
- Constantly comparing their own body parts/image to those of celebrities or peers

The issue of digital enhancement needs to be addressed with young people. Young pre-teens can be particularly gullible, not realising that what they see online in terms of a person's body is not real. There is so much airbrushing, etc. in today's world, young people deserve the space to talk about this and decide what it means to them to be bombarded with so much unreality. Reality TV shows, some of which link in to social media, are actually, to a large extent, fake rather than real. Therefore it is important to talk to your pre-teen and teenage children about this issue on a regular basis so that they remain aware of how manipulated the images they are being bombarded with every day are.

Young people with anorexia nervosa lose weight by restricting their intake of food but that does not mean this disorder is simply about weight. If young people have a weight issue they can engage in a programme of healthy eating and exercise in order to lose weight in a safe way. Anorexia is something different and much more complex than that and young people need to be educated about this fact. Anorexia is never simply about wanting to lose weight. It is a complex mental health issue related to difficult emotions. Going back to the idea of beliefs impacting on thoughts impacting on feelings impacting on behaviours, we can see what can happen in the case of a young girl like Sophie in the example above:

A young person like Sophie is at risk of developing an eating disorder. She feels good when getting 'likes' for her selfies. She begins to think:

- I am attractive to others and that is good.
- When I am thinner, I am more attractive.

Then, at an unconscious level, under the surface, the following beliefs can develop:

- In order to be of worth, I need to be very thin.
- I can control my sense of self-worth by not eating much.

Explain to your children, as discussed previously, that beliefs remain at an unconscious level unless you dig down and explore them and bring them up to the surface. Therefore, they will not be aware of their beliefs automatically and so do not, unless they discover them, have power over how their beliefs ultimately impact on their behaviour.

Using this Case Study to Discuss Mental Health

In discussing this case study with your child, a good place to start would be to ask them if they know anything about eating disorders. Both boys and girls should be engaged in a conversation about this as both boys and girls can develop eating disorders and both need to know how to stay mentally well. Most young people will have heard of the term 'eating disorder'. It is important they know that this is a complex *emotional* disorder and it can be about wanting control just as much as anything else. In talking through the example of what is happening to Sophie, emphasise the following issues:

- Sophie is dealing with the psychological task of identity formation.
- Much of her confidence is coming from an external source.
- Sophie sees her parents dealing with the stress and strain of financial pressure in business and this may impact on her parents' current provision of a secure base.
- Her beliefs are unconscious.

The Psychological Task of Identity Formation

Much attention is given to how a person looks and this focus on appearance as a measure of worth has become so common that young people, unless they have the chance to really pick this idea apart and examine it, just see it as completely normal. But the world hasn't always been like this and other parts of the world are not like this. It's not that long ago that 'selfie' was not even a word. If young people were to imagine a world where there wasn't much attention given to physical appearance they would probably find it hard to even imagine it, but such a place does and can exist.

During adolescence, the psychological task in the mind of the young person is to work out their identity. Self-image can be a big issue for young people as they try to figure themselves out. Many young people are not aware of how sexualised the social media world can be. To be deemed sexually attractive has become synonymous with being liked and this can be the narrow filter through which some young people assess their worth. In exploring the case study of Sophie, the following questions can help your child begin to process their own sense of self-worth as it is developing:

- What do you think about the fact that this is happening for Sophie?
- Do you think she sees a link between her fixation on her appearance and her psychological task of working out her identity?
- Do you think Sophie knows about her psychological task?
- Do you think most people do?
- Does her focus on wanting to be seen as attractive make sense to you?
- If so, why?
- Do you think that a lot of people Sophie's age focus a lot on 'likes' and selfies?
- Why do you think that is?
- Has anything happened to you online that makes you think 'This is me trying to work out my identity'?
- Do you think Sophie is right to focus so much on her weight?
- What do you think it would be like if Sophie didn't care so much what others thought of her?

Internal Versus External Confidence

If a young person is getting most of their confidence from an external source it creates risk, and this is the case with Sophie. It is important to regularly check what feedback your child is getting on their appearance and how that is making them feel. Some parents may think that if their child is very popular and deemed attractive by peers they are not at risk of mental health difficulties, but, as can be seen in Sophie's story, this is not necessarily the case. Sourcing a majority of one's confidence externally puts young people at risk, whether the feedback they are getting is good or bad. So it is important that confidence is something that is brought up regularly in conversation. Here are some questions parents can use to begin the conversation:

- How much of Sophie's confidence comes from an external source, do you think?
- Is that a good thing for her, to have her confidence based on someone else's opinion?

- Do you know how much of your confidence comes from an external source?
- Is it something you keep a check on?
- Why do you think so many young people care so much about how they look?
- Do you think there is a very big emphasis in society on appearance and attractiveness?
- Do you think that's right, to judge a person's worth on their appearance?
- Do you judge people on their appearance/on their selfies?
- On a scale of 1 to 10, if 1 was you didn't care at all and 10 was you cared a lot, how much do you care about the feedback you get for your selfies?
- Do you wish you could care less? (If the answer is yes, you can suggest an exercise involving your child tracking their thoughts when posting a selfie. This is a way for them to begin to explore what they are thinking and why they might believe feedback on that selfie matters so much. Offer to support them to work this out, if they are open to this idea.)

Parental Stress and Its Impact on Secure Base Provision

The environment at home cannot be ignored because the environment at home is one of the factors that Sophie will consider (most likely on an unconscious level) when it comes to talking or not talking about how she is feeling. The environment – the openness that Sophie feels in terms of her parents' support and presence in her world – is either conducive to her sharing her worries with them or not. And while it is not at all the only factor that influences whether Sophie opens up or not, it is likely that if Sophie sees her parents under a lot of strain and stress due to their business she will be less likely to want to burden them with more stress, and may even feel that they are not that interested anyway in how she is feeling. Also, Sophie might not be in the habit of talking about how she feels with her family at home and, because she had mostly felt well, her parents may have seen that type of conversation as unnecessary.

It is important to point out to your child that while they may have ideas about how open or not you would be to supporting them, unless they actually talk to you they won't know if their ideas are true. Point out, using this example, that Sophie could very well be wrong to think her parents wouldn't or couldn't be there for her to lean on; it could just be that they haven't noticed her not feeling ok; they have noticed her not eating but they have felt annoyed rather than concerned about that and, as they have a lot of other things going on, and they are used to her feeling ok, they just aren't aware of her difficulties. This in no way indicates they don't care, even though Sophie may interpret it this way.

Here are some questions you could use to prompt your child to explore their own ideas about their attachment relationship:

- Why do you think Sophie didn't talk to her parents about any of this?
- Do you think maybe she thinks they are too busy to listen?
- Do you think Sophie doesn't want to have someone else know in case they force her to eat?
- What do you think of that idea?
- Do you think Sophie should trust her parents?

You can then talk to your child about whether they know that you would always do your best to support them and would always listen. Ask explicitly if your child ever thinks that you are too busy to listen to them, and be very clear that you are not. Do they think they could trust you to support them? Ask if there has ever been a time when they trusted you with something and you let them down. Encourage an honest answer and reassure them that if they ever told you anything that was going on for them, the thing you would feel most is glad that they were able to trust you and tell you.

Making Unconscious Beliefs Conscious

At an unconscious level, young people who develop eating disorders usually want to be in control of something because certain things in their life seem outside of their control and that doesn't feel good. For Sophie, aspects of her life may seem outside of her control and therefore she may be feeling insecure. Perhaps the financial problems at home make her feel insecure and unsure about the future; perhaps her place within her peer group is something she feels insecure about; or it could be her self-image. Like a lot of other young people, Sophie has developed a need for likes she receives for her selfies as a way to validate her worth. She isn't getting the chance to step back from this situation and reflect on her beliefs, and therefore she is at risk of developing a mental health disorder. Once eating disorders take hold, a person's body image becomes distorted and so can their sense of what is important. Young people battling eating disorders are often loath to give up the control they have over their eating as it is something that, on an unconscious level, makes them feel powerful. Therefore, it is always best to spot the signs early and intervene quickly if that is possible. Using this case study with young people who post selfies on social media is one way to reduce the risk of an obsessional, unhealthy focus on appearance being triggered by their social media use. Focus needs to be placed on beliefs in order to make what is under the surface of their mind known. Asking questions such as those above is a way to make conscious:

- Beliefs the young person has or is developing about themselves
- Beliefs about the way the world is when it comes to emphasising appearance and the way the social media world can reflect this
- Beliefs about how best to mind themselves and their confidence while on social media

In Sophie's situation, it is important that her parents state very clearly that they are worried about her as they see her spending all her time online and not interacting with her friends in a real way. If Sophie is not willing to talk, it may be necessary for her to attend the GP as a first point of contact with a professional. However, if she is willing to talk, it is important that her parents don't tell her what to do but initially explore with her what she is feeling and thinking, why she is so invested in getting likes and what she thinks about her relationship with food currently. If Sophie can see that all of her confidence is being sourced externally, she may be able to shift the balance of this, with support from her parents. She also needs to start eating in order to recover and the idea of developing a relationship with food where you see it as fuel to keep your body and mind going is a simple idea to share with her. Sophie will need to curtail her social media use in order to recover. If she is unwilling to do this, her parents will need to seek outside support.

KNOWING HOW AND WHEN THE FOCUS NEEDS TO BE ON RECOVERY

The above case studies illustrate how things can go wrong for young people online. By going through these case studies with your child, they will be aware that things can go wrong in three main ways:

- When they find themselves in a dangerous or challenging situation because of something they did
- When someone else says or does something that causes them distress
- When their mind is causing them difficulty

In each of these types of scenarios, the young person will need to recover from the difficulty in order to feel fully well again. By having this information, young people will be able to check in with themselves in a more structured way and check if they may need to think about recovery and getting themselves back on track. Sometimes it is really obvious, if something happens suddenly such as in the case of Eugene, that the person has something to recover from. Sometimes however, like in the case of Sophie, the idea of recovery may not be as obvious to the young person themselves. It is essential, therefore, that parents stay tuned in and that young people have the information about these three different types of scenarios that can cause potential harm, so that they are more likely to tune in to how they are feeling. When it comes to staying mentally healthy online, awareness about one's current state of mental well-being is a major part of the picture.

Conclusion

'Whether you think you can, or you think you can't – you're right.'

Henry Ford

Being a Parent in Today's World

Is it possible to keep your child safe on social media? If you think you can, then it becomes true that you can. Every parent has a view on social media and the view you hold is influenced to a large extent by what you believe. Some of you may even still believe that children don't need to be 'kept safe' on social media, although most parents are now coming to realise the importance of staying involved in their children's social media lives, right up until they become adults. According to the National Society for the Prevention for Cruelty to Children in the United Kingdom, social media is contributing to a 14 per cent rise in the numbers of young people engaging in self-harming behaviours because of the pressures and insecurities they feel (Sky News, 9 December 2016). Many more parents than before are becoming aware of research such as this and so the numbers holding onto the belief that young people don't need any support at all with their online life are dwindling.

There are many aspects of the world we live in today that are hugely positive for young people, and that includes the presence of the internet. The internet allows children to learn so much and experience so much. It allows them to connect with people with similar interests from around the world and it is a place where support can be found, if needed. Technological advances have been a powerful force for good and young people benefit in many ways from them, not least by having access to a diversity of learning experiences. Never before have our young been able to access so much information and connect so easily with people from all around the globe who can inform and inspire them. But you need to remain vigilant about the fact that children cannot engage with social media the way we as adults do. The habits of us adults online are very different from those of our children. Children and adolescents are at a completely different level of psychological development to us and so while you can go online and socialise, shop and debate without incident (although some adults too get caught out online, being duped and taken advantage of), your child, because of their developmental stage, absolutely *needs* your support. I am certain of that.

Research published in 2015, called *Kaspersky Lab Study: Children Online*, found that less than a quarter of parents were using parental control software to help restrict their children's activity online. The research, which was carried out by a research company called B2B International and the leading US internet safety company, Kaspersky Lab, also found that only a third of parents (in the US, Europe and the Asia-Pacific region) worry that their children could be exposed to inappropriate or explicit content online. In the context of a Senate inquiry in Canberra, Australia, in 2016, which found that 'children as young as five are sexually abusing their peers after being exposed to pornography', this belief about not having to worry about what children view online, and the possible consequences of that, seems negligent or, at best, naïve (Tillet, 2016). Whatever your own beliefs regarding harm or danger online, be clear that it is your own beliefs that influence, more than anything else, your action or inaction in relation to your child's online safety. Would you give your kids the keys to the family car and let them work out how to drive down the road for themselves? The answer is most likely no because beliefs about the dangers of driving without having any clue as to how to manage that activity are well set in our minds and have been for some time. But cars have been around a lot longer than social media has been and so our beliefs have had a chance to bed down. Social media and the internet have most definitely complicated the job of parenting. But complicated jobs can still be done well, once we know how.

Giving your child the message early on that you like being in their company, and you believe them to be very precious, impacts in a hugely positive way on your child and your relationship with them, and it is part of the foundation for helping them manage online life too as they grow. As your child grows and goes through the teenage years they will most likely want increasing amounts of time away from you. This shift towards independence is normal and good and it can be useful in supporting them to manage life online to talk about this increasing independence ahead of time. If you have a conversation with your child about this aspect of their development you are normalising the gradual separation and taking charge of how your relationship manages to navigate this tricky time. It's an opportunity for you to say that despite them growing up and becoming more independent you will always be there for them, for any reason and at any time, to give support. This really matters when it comes to their online life, even though it seems so basic. It matters that you allow them more independence as they grow, and set the scene early for negotiation being an expected part of how this increasing independence is managed. You need to be confident that you have prepared your child well to manage in the environment of social media. Filters can be placed on devices but that isn't enough to ensure they will be safe. Be comfortable expecting your child to do preparatory work. Treat it like learning to drive: they need to learn the ropes, prepare, do the work. Then gradually they will be allowed out, with support, to drive.

THE STORIES WE HOLD

Stories play an important part in our lives and we tell ourselves stories all of the time, even if we're not aware that we are doing it. We tell ourselves stories about who cares, stories about who has let us down and why, stories about the way people are, the way the world is, how the future might likely be. In a way, these stories become your truth. The stories shape your reality. So what story do you hold currently about social media?

Social Media

It is worth stepping back for a moment and taking the time to tune into how you really feel about social media. Knowing social media as an adult is only one aspect of the story. Knowing how different your child's stage of development and needs are is another part of the story you now have too. Here are three main stories or dominant truths about social media you might hold; each of them are fuelled by different beliefs and they each lead to a different set of actions:

- The 'social media is harmless' story – which can lead to ambivalence, which can then lead to inaction and your child not being supported well online.
- The 'kids will always be two steps ahead of me where social media is concerned' story – which can lead to anxiety or resignation, which can lead to inaction and burying your head in sand.
- The 'I can take a lead on this and support my child to stay safe and well on social media' story – which leads to confidence, which leads to confident action, good communication and forward planning.

The 'Social Media Is Harmless' Story

Scarily, this story is dominant. Most parents use social media and therefore form a view of it from that perspective. And for some parents, it really can be hard to see any danger with it for their child, especially when their own personal use of it is causing no harm to them. Your child absolutely needs to be prepared for social media use and they need your support while on social media. If not, your child could end up in very difficult situations and dealing with difficult emotions. If you hold this story currently, challenge your beliefs. If this story remains unchallenged and in your unconscious mind your child is not getting the level of support and guidance they require. Social media may not cause harm but it is best to err on the side of caution, knowing that it could.

The 'Parents Are Always Playing Catch-Up' Story

This is a story that gets told and re-told; when it comes to social media, parents are always playing catch-up. It gets repeated and then people believe it to be true. But just because this is a story that is talked about does not make it necessarily true. Parents don't have to always be in the position of playing catch-up. You can take a lead. In terms of what you believe, it matters that you check if what you believe leads to action or inaction. The story you hold impacts how you feel and how you behave. It is important to look closely at all the stories you tell yourself about your life, your children's lives and the relationship you have with and ideas you have about social media. It is important when it comes to parenting around social media that the story you hold and believe is not disempowering. To tell yourself you are always playing catch-up will never put you in a place where you feel empowered. And empowerment matters as it leads directly to confident action.

The 'I Can Work to Keep My Child Safe on Social Media' Story

This story is 100 per cent empowering and leads to confident action. It's also the story I believe firmly to be true. Once you know about psychological development in adolescence, once you know how to source confidence internally and can explain it to your child, once you understand the importance of attachment and have explained to your child how to manage difficult emotions and how to recover when things go wrong, you are on track to keeping your child safe and well.

It is important that you feel comfortable and familiar with the steps in this book to really own the story of being fully confident about how to go forward and keep your child safe. And even with full confidence, sometimes things happen that can cause your confidence as a parent to spill out. That's perfectly normal. But at least by knowing how to mind your own confidence (as well as training your child in how to mind theirs), you can build resilience and strength in the role you play as mentor for your child too. Getting clarity on the following issues can help you hold onto your confidence too:

- The link between knowledge about psychological development and confidence
- Your view on objectification
- Considering the age of the child
- Introducing the topic of pornography to young people
- Introducing knowledge of adult social media sites to young people

The Link between Knowledge about Psychological Development and Confidence

Even if your child does not know what is going with their own mind's development, as a parent if you have this knowledge you are in a strong position in terms of understanding your child and offering them support. You can be tuned in to what is going on, even on an unconscious level, with your child. Then you can impart this knowledge to your child as they begin adolescence. Your child will then have this knowledge for themselves to help them understand any feelings, fears and motivations they are dealing with. Children of eleven or twelve years of age can understand the concept of identity formation if it is explained to them. Children who are a little older, thirteen or fourteen years, will be in a better position to understand more fully all of what happens in the mind of an adolescent. For example, the concepts of identity formation, the movement from concrete to abstract thinking and the move psychologically away from parents all make more sense the older an adolescent gets. It can be a huge relief for young people to know what they are facing in their mind. Every child is different but as a guide I would suggest giving your child information about their own psychological development in stages. First, the identity formation task can be explained and discussed before your child starts to use social media (which for me, equates to at least age twelve as I would not see younger children as being able to handle social media before that age). Then, after they have grasped the basic concept, the other aspects of psychological development can be explained in a gradual way over a few months to them. Knowing about this developmental stage should help your confidence.

Your View on Objectification

As your child begins adolescence, they need to be supported in developing an awareness of and an opinion about the process of objectification. If you are aware of and have an opinion about objectification yourself this will provide clarity on the position you are speaking from and should help you talk about it more confidently. You do not have to have a particular opinion about objectification (you may feel it's quite ok to objectify adults but not children, or you may feel strongly that it's not ok to objectify anybody). You don't need to share your view about objectification with your child. You can say that objectification is an aspect of what happens in the world today and it is important that your child makes up their own mind about it over time. If you want to share your view, then do. But you can give an opinion on the objectifying of children and teens rather than adults, if that fits better. By having this conversation you can influence your child's mind, especially if they are still young when the topic is introduced.

One way to introduce the topic of objectification is to ask your child, at age eleven, twelve or thirteen, if they know what the difference between an object and a person is. You can ask if they think it's ever ok to treat a person or see a person as an object. If they say yes, then the discussion could lead on to talking about how treating someone like an object means that you don't have empathy for that person or see them as having feelings. You can then ask if there would be anything risky or bad about doing this.

If you introduce the topic for discussion later on in adolescence, for example with a young person who is fifteen or sixteen, the conversation could also include some discussion about whether the selfie culture has led to people seeing others in their selfie posts like objects. Gaining awareness about objectification can be challenging for young people and yet it is so important that they learn about this process and how it can happen. By becoming clear about your own personal views, it will be easier for you to helpfully engage in conversations about objectification with your child.

Considering the Age of the Child

As a rule of thumb, as soon as children are old enough to know what social media is, they are old enough to start preparing for using it. Understanding confidence and its sources and developing secure attachment is work that can begin to be really focused on with children from the age of eight or nine. As they reach ten or eleven, a more specific focus on where exactly their confidence is coming from, how to manage difficult emotions and beginning to understand their own psychological development can become part of the preparatory work, although these age categorisations are only a guide. You can plan these conversations and have a topic for discussion. They can be named conversations about preparing for social media, thus giving your child the message that:

- Social media is something they need to be prepared for
- Their parents can do the preparatory work with them

Once you are confident about understanding the steps involved in doing the work, your child will see that you know how to support them in their social media life.

Introducing the Topic of Pornography to Young People

In relation to bringing up conversations about pornography, it is true that young people are accessing pornography online at a young age but it is also true that some young children at age ten or eleven may not have heard the term 'pornography' before. Therefore, you may be wary of introducing this topic to your child in case they don't yet know what it is. If this is a situation you find yourself in, bringing up a conversation about objectification can be an alternative route. This is an age-appropriate way to begin talking to children of ten or eleven about an aspect of pornography that is of central importance. By talking about objectification rather than using the term 'pornography' you are introducing a concept that relates to what happens with pornography. In order to engage with pornography, the viewer will likely see the participants are sexual objects. So to have a conversation about the fact that sometimes people view others as objects can be enough for children of that age. When they are twelve and understand more, the conversation can develop to how people sometimes see others as sexual objects, rather than just objects, and you can point out that people sometimes do this without even being aware that it is happening. Gradually the young person will become more aware and then if/when they do see something pornographic, they will have a better context for understanding it, perhaps being able to see how the people in the porn are in fact being viewed as objects, rather than them just simply being overwhelmed with sexual arousal.

Introducing Knowledge of Adult Social Media Sites to Young People

Before young people start to use social media, they should have some knowledge about how to manage difficult feelings (Step Four) and they should also have some awareness that things can go wrong (Step Five). In working through these steps with your child, it is very important that information about adult social media sites, information about how to access these sites and the names of these sites are not shared until you are quite sure that this is information that your child already has or is likely to have access to from peers. By the time young people are fifteen years old it is highly likely that they will be aware of the existence of some adult social media sites and at this age it would be appropriate to work through all the case studies outlined in this book at your own discretion. Before this age, however, it is important that you are careful about the language you use and the terms you use when discussing the internet generally with your child. If you wish to check if your child has heard of an adult social media site, you can ask them if they ever hear anyone in school talking about social media sites that are not for their age group. This could form part of a more general conversation about what sites are the most popular among their peers and about how accessing a site that is not for their age group is highly dangerous. You should always be totally clear on and aware of the names of the social media sites your child is using (until adulthood). Questions such as the following can prompt discussion:

- What social media sites are the most popular at the moment?
- What social media sites are your friends using?
- Does anyone ever talk about social media sites that are not meant for their age group?

By introducing the conversation topic in this way, you not only have the opportunity to let your child know that accessing a site that is not for their age group can be very damaging and dangerous, but also that you are knowable about social media sites. This is a good message to give your child. It tells them that their parents are not playing catch up. It tells them that you are 'in the know' about what can go on.

***

Social media has become a filter through which many young people are working out their own sense of who they are. You are in a key position to support your child to stay safe and mentally well online, and so it is important to tune into your own confidence. And in particular, it is good to be aware of how much confidence you feel about parenting around social media. Confidence can be threatened for adults just as it can be for children; if something bad or unexpected happens to you or even if you are dealing with a teenager who communicates disrespectfully and seems to always push your boundaries your confidence can take a hit. I have met brilliant parents who cannot understand how things went wrong for their child online, but tough times happen in life and tough times can happen online too. For too long now, parents have been unsure what to do to keep their children safe, resilient and strong. So let's own this story and this truth: our children can be safe and mentally well on social media – we just need to stay alert and involved, and follow five easy steps.

References

American Heritage Dictionary (2016) *The American Heritage Dictionary of the English Language*, fifth edition, https://ahdictionary.com/.

Beck, J. (2011) *Cognitive Behavior Therapy: Basics and Beyond*, second edition, New York: Guilford Press.

Bowlby, J. (1990) *Child Care and the Growth of Love*, London: Penguin

Erikson, E. and Erikson, J. (1997) *The Life Cycle Completed*, New York: W.W. Norton.

Kaspersky Lab and B2B International (2015) *Kaspersky Lab Study: Children Online*, Version 1.0, March, https://securelist.com/files/2015/03/Kaspersky_Lab_KSN_report_Children_Online_eng.pdf, Moscow: Kaspersky Lab.

Ofcom (2015) *Children and Parents: Media Use and Attitudes Report 2015*, November, https://www.ofcom.org.uk/research-and-data/media-literacy-research/children/children-parents-nov-15, London: Ofcom.

Rao, G. and Madan, A. (2013) 'A Study Exploring the Link between Attachment Styles and Social Networking Habits of Adolescents in Urban Bangalore', *International Journal of Scientific and Research Publications*, Vol. 3, No. 1, pp. 1–12.

Tillet, A. (2016) 'Children as Young as Five Driven by Porn', *West Australian*, 29 February, https://thewest.com.au/news/australia/children-as-young-as-five-driven-by-porn-ng-ya-326654.

FURTHER READING

Allen, J., Porter, M. and McFarland, C. (2007) 'The Relation of Attachment Security to Adolescents' Parental and Peer Relationships, Depression and Externalizing Behaviour', *Child Development*, Vol. 78, No. 4, pp. 1222–1239.

American Osteopathic Association (2014) 'Top Five Warning Signs of Internet Pornography Addiction', *American Osteopathic Association*, 27 October, https://www.osteopathic.org/inside-aoa/news-and-publications/media-center/2014-news-releases/Pages/OMED-2014-top-five-warning-signs-of-internet-pornography-addiction.aspx.

Baker, N. (2013) 'Teenagers Should Be Warned on Sexting Dangers', *Irish Examiner*, 23 March.

Burr, V. (2003) *Social Constructionism*, London and New York: Routledge.

Catlett, J. (2015) 'Understanding Anxious Attachment – Part 2: Avoidant Attachment', *Psych Alive*, 13 February, http://www.psychalive.org/anxious-avoidant-attachment/?utm_content=buffer51e4c&utm_medium=social&utm_source=twitter.com&utm_campaign=buffer.

Curwen, B., Palmer, S. and Ruddell, P. (2003) *Brief Cognitive Behaviour Therapy*, London: Sage.

Cyr, B.A., Berman, S. and Smith, M. (2014) 'The Role of Communication Technology in Adolescent Relationships and Identity Development', *Child and Youth Care Forum*, Vol. 44, No. 1, pp. 79–92.

De Angelis, T. (2007) 'Web Pornography's Effect on Children', *American Psychological Association*, Vol. 38, No. 10, p. 50, http://www.apa.org/monitor/nov07/webporn.aspx.

Fortune, J. (2013) 'The Warping of Our Teens' View of Sex', *Irish Independent*, 21 October.

Galotti, K. (2011) *Cognitive Development: Infancy Through Adolescence*, London: Sage.

Giles, D. and Maltby, J. (2004) 'The Role of Media Figures in Adolescent Development: Relations between Autonomy, Attachment, and Interest in Celebrities', *Personality and Individual Differences*, Vol. 36, No. 4, pp. 813–822.

Hitti, A., Mulvey, K.L. and Killen, M. (2014) 'Social Exclusion in Adolescence', in R.J.R Levesque (ed.), *Encyclopedia of Adolescence*, New York: Springer-Verlay.

Holden, L. (2014) 'Teaching Children to Protect Themselves Online', *Irish Times*, 1 April.

Irish Examiner (2015) 'Web Porn Blamed for Child-on-Child Sex Attacks', 25 May.

Irish Examiner (2015) 'Porn Helps Feed Sex Addiction', 23 November.

Khan, S., Gagne, M., Yang, L. and Shapka, J. (2016) 'Exploring the Relationship between Adolescents' Self-Concept and Their Offline and Online Social Worlds', *Computers in Human Behaviour*, Vol. 55, No. B, pp. 940–945.

Margolies, L. (2015) 'Teens and Internet Pornography', *Psych Central*, 10 December, https://psychcentral.com/lib/teens-and-internet-pornography/.

McCormack, A. (2015) 'Social Media, Safety and Sexts: Boundaries and Breaking Points for Teenagers', *Irish Times*, 27 October.

Owens, E., Behun, R., Manning, J. and Reid, R. (2012) 'The Impact of Internet Pornography on Adolescents: A Review of the Research', *Sexual Addiction & Compulsivity*, Vol. 19, Nos. 1–2, pp. 99–122.

Perraudin, F. (2014) 'Social Porn: Why People Are Sharing Their Sex Lives Online', *The Guardian*, 18 March.

Samson, O. (2016) 'Parents Lack Visibility, Control over Children's Online Activity', *Business Mirror*, 11 November.

Smith, V. (2014) 'Four in Ten Infants Lack Strong Attachment', *Science Daily*, 27 March, https://www.sciencedaily.com/releases/2014/03/140327123540.htm.

Theran, S., Newberg, E. and Gleason, T. (2010) 'Adolescent Girls' Parasocial Interactions with Media Figures', *Journal of Genetic Psychology*, Vol. 171, No. 3, pp. 270–277.

Whiteman, H. (2015) 'Social Media: How Does It Affect Our Mental Health and Well-Being?', *Medical News Today*, 10 June, http://www.medicalnewstoday.com/articles/275361.php.